JUST KEEP
BREATHING

JUST KEEP BREATHING

A Shocking Exposé of Real Letters You
Never Imagined a Generation Was Writing

REGGIE DABBS AND
JOHN DRIVER

W PUBLISHING GROUP

AN IMPRINT OF THOMAS NELSON

Published in Nashville, Tennessee, by W Publishing Group, an imprint of Thomas Nelson.

Thomas Nelson titles may be purchased in bulk for educational, business, fund-raising, or sales promotional use. For information, please e-mail SpecialMarkets@ThomasNelson.com.

The stories told in this book are based on true events, but there are certain names, persons, characters, places, and dates that have been changed so that the persons and characters portrayed bear no resemblance to persons actually living or dead. Names and facts from stories contained in this book have been changed, but the emotional and sexual struggles are true as related to the author through personal interviews, letters, or e-mails. Permission has been granted for the use of real names and correspondence.

Library of Congress Cataloging-in-Publication Data

Names: Dabbs, Reggie.
Title: Just keep breathing : a shocking expose of real letters you never
    imagined a generation was writing / Reggie Dabbs and John Driver.
Description: Nashville : W Publishing Group, an imprint of Thomas Nelson,
    2016.
Identifiers: LCCN 2015024785 | ISBN 9780718077198 (trade paper)
Subjects: LCSH: Bullying in schools—United States. | Dabbs,
    Reggie—Correspondence.
Classification: LCC LB3013.32 D33 2016 | DDC 371.5/8—dc23 LC record
    available at http://lccn.loc.gov/2015024785

Printed in the United States of America
HB 01.26.2022

Contents

Enter the Inkwell: A Prologue   1

Chapter 1: Unfixable and Invaluable

Letter 1: *I Was Raped, Bullied, and I Wontto Die . . .*   25
    but No One Cares

Letter 2: *If I Was Meant to Live, Why the H*** Would*   30
    I Want to Die?

Letter 3: *I Will Not Let the Bullies Win*   33

Exhale 1: *Could All this Be True?*   38

Signature 1: *Leave Your Own Impression*   45

Chapter 2: Roles and Holes

Letter 4: *You Saved My Life, Dad!*   51

Letter 5: *My Dad Died, and I Blamed Myself*   57

Letter 6: *I Will Be Great!*   61

Exhale 2: *Spoons and Shovels*   64

Signature 2: *Leave Your Own Impression*   71

Chapter 3: Bullies and Backstories

Letter 7: *I Joined a Gang, and Now They Want to Kill Me!*   77

Letter 8: *Two Teens in Australia Have Jumped in Front of*   81
     Trains . . . Help!

Letter 9: *How Do I Erase the Names: Whore, Lesbian,*   83
     Pothead, Alcoholic?

Exhale 3: *Bully Backstories*   86

Signature 3: *Leave Your Own Impression*   93

Chapter 4: Quality and Quantity

Letter 10: *I Was Called Stupid, Dumb, or Stupid F***ing*   99
     Ginger 307 Times

Letter 11: *People Call Me a Babykiller*   102

Letter 12: *My Dad Says I Don't Deserve a Birthday*   107

Exhale 4: *Silencing Mouths or Changing Minds*   111

Signature 4: *Leave Your Own Impression*   119

Chapter 5: Action and Inaction

Letter 13: *I Wrapped a Cord Around My Neck and*   125
     Almost Jumped

Letter 14: *All My Family Says, "Kill Yourself"*   129

Letter 15: *I Want to Move Away and Grow*   132

Exhale 5: *Problem or Solution?*   138

Signature 5: *Leave Your Own Impression*   147

Chapter 6: Pain and Potential

Letter 16: *My Grandpa Sexually Harassed Me and Killed Himself*   153

Letter 17: *Somebody Does Really Care!*   158

Letter 18: *My Mom Almost Took My Life*   162

Exhale 6: *Dominoes, Depression, and Family*   166

Signature 6: *Leave Your Own Impression*   174

Chapter 7: Entitlement and Empowerment

Letter 19: *I Was Almost Aborted, and My Dad Left*   179

Letter 20: *I Lost My Large Intestine . . . and I Want to Lose My Life Too*   183

Letter 21: *My Name Is Unneeded (written just months before a shooting at her school)*   186

Exhale 7: *Hidden Superheroes*   188

Signature 7: *Leave Your Own Impression*   195

Endless Ink: An Epilogue   199

Notes   205

About the Authors   207

Enter the Inkwell: A Prologue

Throughout my life i have been beaten by foster parents, by family's boyfriends, by people I don't even know. I grew up in pure hell and torture. I lost my mom for 5 years due to her love for alcohol and not her own kids.

I have been bullied and sexually harrassed.

I have been kidnapped and raped.

—"Madison"

My boyfriend and his little brother and friend killed thmself. It will be 2 years ago tomarrow. I get abused and hurt so much, no one cares.

—"Rachel"

When I turned 12 years old, I was initiated into a gang. . . . They're looking for me and want to kill me, but I guess it's what I deserve, right?

—"Carlos"

Thank you so much for making me stop and think for a minute. Because to be honest with you, I was planning on leaving everything behind. When i woke up friday morning, i decided that i was done. And Friday after school, nobody was going to have to deal with me anymore.

—"Lauren"

On Your Mark . . .

These are but a few snippets from letters contained in the pages to come. They are real, and they are worth your time. However, we really believe you need to understand who we are and why we are doing this before diving into the letters. Thanks for giving us just a few pages to set the stage for what is to come.

SHOES

Right now, somewhere on this planet, the soles of an unknown pair of shoes just touched the hot pavement outside an unsuspecting school. Right foot. Left foot. Step after fateful step, they move in stride toward a glass-laden door . . . a door separating the outside world from our very hearts. For inside this building is the breathing core of all we cherish and care for most deeply. Inside this school is the next generation.

They are your friends. Your students. Your brother. Your sister. Your childhood sweetheart. The ex-boyfriend you once loved but now hate. Your mom, who is a teacher. Your children. Your husband. They may even be you—just another kid swimming from class to class in a sea of high school humanity.

They are millions of people, and they mean everything to us. That is why these shoes fast approaching the front door of this school are so important. They keep some people up at night with worry—dread, the unthinkable, the unknown, the possibility. The—dare I say it—*probability* of tragedies to come.

In 1998, in Jonesboro, Arkansas, the shoes were sneakers of two young boys, eleven and thirteen years old, who pulled a fire alarm to lure hundreds of innocent students and teachers out of the school doors and into their crosshairs. Five kids and one teacher died. In 1999, at Columbine High School in Colorado, the shoes were combat boots of two teenagers geared up with assault rifles who gunned down thirteen people.

5

And in 2012, at Sandy Hook Elementary School in Connecticut, the shoes were familiar—filled by the son of one of the victims. Twenty-six people, most of them very young children, lost their precious lives that horrific day. These are not even close to a full list of all the tragedies that have happened on school grounds, even if they are the most recognizable ones.

Right now somewhere on this planet, the soles of an unknown pair of shoes just touched the hot pavement outside an unsuspecting school.

But the truth is this book is not really about school violence or the tragedies that exist *inside the schools*. It is actually a life-sized glimpse into the realities that exist *inside the people*, many of whom we have met in schools.

Just to make a point though, the truth remains that each of these violent school tragedies began with a pair of shoes laced upon feet walking an intentional path toward a door. And each day, each of us wonders what shoes—and what kind of people filling them—are walking toward the door. We have so much to lose. So much to dread. Today is no different.

That pair of shoes on the hot pavement is still walking toward those glass doors. This is not a drill or a metaphor. I mean this quite literally. As you read these words, this is happening— right now.

These particular shoes are size thirteen. They are laced onto the feet of a man dressed in dark clothes, mid- to late forties. He pushes the button outside the door, ringing his request to enter. The front office assistant looks through the window. He is a large black man with a shaved head and gray goatee. And he is carrying a small, narrow case in his hand.

She pushes the button to unlock the door and the intimidating man waltzes right past security with no resistance. He is now in the middle of our hearts. Right where so much damage has been done. So much tragedy inflicted.

His plan is obviously premeditated. He immediately walks to where the largest group of students is gathered. They are loud, unassuming, and unaware of what is about to happen. The man pauses and unzips the case. He reaches inside and pulls out something long, shiny, and metallic. He stands before the students and points the object directly at them.

They don't stand a chance. His weapon of choice: a tenor saxophone. His name: Reggie Dabbs.

Reggie's shoes have walked on every continent over the past twenty-five years, and what he has seen and heard on his long journey into your backyard is nothing short of shocking. He walks into our schools because he is invited to share his incredible story with millions of people. We figure it is high time that you hear *their* stories as well.

It is time to explore our own backyards. These are just a few of their real stories.

HOW FACEBOOK BECAME
OUR BOOK

My name is John Driver, and the words you are about to read will be unique, to say the least. Working as a public school teacher, a community youth mentor, and in various counseling roles, the past fifteen years have brought across my path some incredible and often tragic stories. But few stories have ever affected me more than the story of my good friend Reggie.

His shoes walked into my office one day, and a conversation ensued that found Reggie and I writing a book together about his amazing story. It was released in 2011 under the title of *Reggie: You Can't Change Your Past, but You Can Change Your Future.* The process of writing and working with Reggie so closely led us to work together on other projects, one of which you are reading right now.

Another key project of ours was to better establish Reggie's social media presence so he could communicate better with the people he was trying to reach. He had a personal Facebook "profile" with five thousand "friends" and more than thirteen thousand "friend requests." Yikes! And since at the time Facebook did not allow a personal "profile" to have more than five thousand "friends," we knew we needed to create a new Facebook "page" for Reggie.

That was easier said than done. A simple search across Facebook revealed about five Reggie Dabbs "pages" started by people we had never met. Some even claimed they were Reggie himself, which was pretty dangerous since people often share, as you will soon read, some extremely delicate information with Reggie. All told, Reggie's unofficial "pages" already had about fifteen thousand "fans" (which is what they were called before Facebook switched to "likes" instead).

I contacted Facebook many, many times in an effort to reach out to the owners and "followers" of these "pages," but it was hopeless. We did not want to lose our connection to so many people, but it was just too risky. We shut down those "pages" and started from scratch back at just one solitary "like"—me.

Fast forward several years, and the official Reggie Dabbs Facebook "page" had more than 120,000 "likes," plus more than thirty thousand followers on Twitter. These numbers continue to grow. This is incredible, but something unexpected has accompanied these thousands of "followers": thousands of personal "messages" from them. Early on, Facebook did not allow "messages" to come from "fans" of a "page" to the owners of the "page," but when they changed that policy, the floodgates opened.

We have received thousands of messages from thousands of people all across the planet. Some are from Facebook while others are e-mails or even handwritten letters. Some simply say thanks for coming to their schools, but others pour out their hearts about the sobering realities of life they are facing. Suicidal thoughts. Sexual abuse. Relationship crises. Depression. The issues are endless.

As an educator and someone who has worked with youth and young adults in crisis for years, these stories made my head explode. What were we supposed to do with all of these? How could we ever answer them all, much less help them through their problems? Were we liable for the information? Whom were we supposed to call or report to when we received a Facebook "message" from some kid in trouble living on a mountain in Indonesia or in a suburb in Australia?

It was overwhelming, to say the least. And though we answered and helped as many as we could, it felt like we were trying to clear out a rock quarry one pebble at a time. Keep in mind that all the while, both of us were still speaking and working with people in person. Needless to say, our efforts felt as if they fell extremely short.

Then it hit us—write a book—a short book. Let their voices and stories be heard, but also answer them. The idea of the book was not to be impersonal, but to be *more* personal to more people because for every letter we have used here, there are two hundred others we did not include. This way everyone who has written to us in search of hope, wisdom, or just someone to listen can hear our hearts (and maybe even a little wisdom) in the pages of this book.

But this all begs another question: What's the deal with this Reggie guy, and why do hundreds of thousands of people line up to pour out their hearts to him? Great question. And although this is not really a book about Reggie himself, I should probably introduce you to him for it all to make sense. The easiest way to do this is to drop you directly into the very place that most frequently causes people to gravitate to Reggie—a school or event where he is speaking.

I GOT YO' BACK!

The best way to understand what happens when Reggie's shoes cross the path of an unsuspecting group of people is to look him up on YouTube. You have to see it to believe it. Join the millions who already have, and go watch for yourself.

Disrespectful gang members. Eye-rolling cheerleaders. Cackling middle school students. Stuffy administrators. I kid you not when I say it does not matter who is present. From his first word, Reggie instantaneously captivates any room of any size. The results are uncontrollable bouts of unrestrained laughter followed immediately by silence and more tears than you can measure in a science lab beaker.

As soon as the microphone touches Reggie's lips, he has the room spellbound. He usually opens by telling them to clap for the black man who just got them out of class. They clap.

He usually opens by telling them to clap for the black man who just got them out of class.

Black man? Doesn't sound very politically correct? Get used to disappointment. He tells them that no matter what their race, everybody is just a shade of chocolate—white chocolate, dark chocolate, or milk chocolate. As Reggie would say, it doesn't matter because all chocolate is good. They laugh.

From there, he somehow jumps straight to telling them he knows what it feels like to think your life is worthless because he was born as the result of a twenty-dollar bill. His desperate and abandoned teenage mother slept with a man who paid her twenty dollars so she could buy food to feed her other three babies, who were living with her in an abandoned chicken coop.

Just like that. Silence. Tears. Change.

No games. No tricks. Just a man with a real story and a real heart. A gifted saxophonist and a hilarious storyteller, in about five minutes flat, Reggie has an entire school, full of thugs, jocks, and hearts-hard-as-rocks, holding one another's hands high in the air and singing "I Believe I Can Fly" at the top of their lungs. Even the teachers and principals join the chorus as a school full of fighting, failure, and frustration just a few minutes earlier now sways together in almost perfect harmony.

Reggie has spent the past twenty-five years doing exactly what I just described to you, telling his story to anyone who will listen. And listen they do—by the millions. Though it is a hard title to verify, many media sources have called him the number one public school speaker in the world.

It is not a title he is very concerned about. He is much more interested in the actual people in those schools. And even though he also speaks to stadiums full of tens of thousands of people at many other events internationally, his heart still beats for that one kid in that one rural school that no one else seems to even notice. That's why he comes to schools, plays his sax, and tells his story.

There are a few key words Reggie often repeats that capture the energy of these moments. He has the crowd sing these words at certain points in the songs he plays. He even makes the teachers rap these words as the kids laugh in pure joy over the whole spectacle. Anyone who has ever been to a Reggie event knows those words very well. It is Reggie's catchphrase.

I Got Yo' Back! These are more than just four words to get a crowd pumped. We also believe they are a promise of sort—a vow to listen and to speak up for those who cannot or will not always speak for themselves.

This is a book of their words—words the writers did not know when they wrote them would be published someday. Their identities and locations have been changed to keep them safe and anonymous, but these are their stories—real stories of real people who seriously need someone to have their backs.

CATCH OUR DRIFT; CATCH
THEIR BREATH

It is our hope that this book will provide hope to those who have written to us, as well as the many who have not had the opportunity, ability, or courage to do so. But if I'm being honest, what you are about to read is an intimidating body of work. It is overwhelming to try to help people at their points of crisis *and* give wisdom and resources to others who are helping those around them in similar situations.

So here are a few items of importance that will set the boundaries for what we are going to attempt to do and not do in the coming pages.

The letters are the stars. We want you to hear the voices of this generation as they are speaking. For this reason we have not edited all of their grammatical mistakes. You will even hear a few curse words here and there—and when you read their stories, you will understand why. Since this book will be read in both the public arena and public schools, we have amended some of the language. We have also changed names and replaced dates, school names, and locations with Xs to protect identities, but our hope is that you will enter the real world of some real people you never may have heard otherwise. They are not as far away as you might think. They may be on your soccer team, in your class, in your house—or even in your mirror.

We are not fixing people. I will cover this concept

more in depth in chapter 1. We are dealing with some pretty crazy stuff . . . life and death stuff. Reggie and I will offer a few words in response, but these words are not meant to fix everything. So if it feels like they fall a bit short, that is because they certainly do. Any words fall short when we are dealing with suicide, abuse, and other major crises. But keep reading because even though our few words will not fix everything, all is not lost.

This book is not exhaustive. I mean that it will not cover every issue that our society is facing in complete detail. That would require a thousand libraries instead of a single book. In fact, we have written this book to be a bit short on purpose, mainly because of the varied audience and age groups who will read it. It is not a textbook; it is exposure and encouragement.

Reggie's responses to the letters are real and personal. This book is laid out in chapters, each containing three letters. Each letter is followed by a real response from Reggie. In some cases, the initial response you read from Reggie was written in real time, via e-mail or Facebook. In other cases, Reggie's direct response to a letter appears for the first time in this book. Either way, Reggie's answers focus on responding to the actual person writing the letter. Some are short, and others are more thorough. In some cases, when multiple messages were sent, you can see the original back and forth conversation between Reggie and the individual.

Note that sometimes Reggie will repeat himself or simply offer a word of encouragement. This is by design because we are actually answering real people as if their letters are the only ones. As we will discuss, there are some things we all need to hear more than once.

Reggie's answers focus on responding to the actual person writing the letter.

Our main goal is to keep them breathing another day. As I said before, we are not going to fix everybody, nor are we attempting to do so. One of the repeated things you will hear from Reggie is the challenge to just keep breathing another day. That is our main takeaway: to keep people from giving up on life and ending it (or someone else's) before they have a chance to actually live it. Tomorrow may not end the crisis, but it does contain life if we can just survive until it comes. If life ends today, then tomorrow's life will never be reached. We are focusing on today and the idea that empowering people to choose to keep breathing another day gives all of us hope for what can happen tomorrow. It is a simple approach to an extremely complex group of issues.

Though we discuss this concept in much greater detail later, do not succumb to the temptation to consider such an endeavor shallow or ineffective. You may be saying to yourself, *Really? Shouldn't your objective be a bit more significant or permanent than just keeping them breathing another day?* If that thought crossed your mind, keep reading—this book is for you.

We will offer ten Breathable Moments along the way. These are short phrases designed to stick with you long after you have put away this book. Each one offers an observation or a snippet of wisdom that you can remember and use as you either continue to keep catching your own breath, or as you strive to help others around you keep catching theirs another day.

Each chapter concludes with an Exhale from John. Since keeping people breathing is our focus, I have written sections at the end of each chapter called Exhales. I will observe and comment on the letters per chapter, as well as Reggie's responses. Exhales are designed to help friends, parents, other family members, and educators—and anyone else who is simply conscientiously concerned about helping those around them—find perspective and direction in moments when someone near to them is dealing with the issues presented in this book.

You can leave your own signature in this book. After every Exhale you will find a Signature page, where you can leave your own impressions by exploring questions and ideas from the letters, Reggie's responses, and the Exhales. This is a great place to dig deeper as an individual or to engage in a group discussion about the issues in your own lives and communities.

YOUR SHOES

Now that the pen is sufficiently inked, let's get to it. The pages to come will cover many things written by pens of many people; but mostly, this is a book about shoes. It is not just about schools. It is not just motivational jargon. It is not just for teachers, neither is it just for parents. It is not just for students or their friends.

This is not a book just about tragic stories, one that brings you down so low you cannot see how our society can ever climb out of the hole we are in. You should not need a pick-me-up after reading it. With all this book *is not*, we trust that it *will be* an exposé that will not only open your eyes, but also open your hearts to hope.

As I said, this is a book about shoes—well, sort of. Most everyone you see walking is wearing shoes. Thus, this is a book about everyone, and even more so about the people filling those shoes we so easily dismiss, overlook, or ignore. So no matter what compartment of your brain you instinctively try to squeeze this book into, please don't. That's what got us here in the first place. We have put people and their stories into neat, conclusive, arm's-length, media-friendly shoe boxes for too long.

We are not writing this to overstimulate you with statistics or sad tales. We are not offering up another book about all that's "wrong with kids and society these days." In fact, if you see the stories of kids and think this is a kids' book, you are missing the forest for the trees. The traffic for the cars. The very nose on your face. You are missing the fact that this book is about you. Your life. Your family. Your community.

Your shoes.

Unfixable and Invaluable

CHAPTER 1

Unfixable and
Invaluable

LETTER 1:
I WAS RAPED, BULLIED, AND I WONTTO DIE . . . BUT NO ONE CARES

"RACHEL"

Dear Reggie,

I know you probably wont get this. But im at the XX and i wontto die. I always wontto die. I cut so much. I have had over 15 stitches. I have overdosed over 3 times. But God doesnt let me die. He wont let me. I dont wontto be here. I get pushed in the lockers at school. I get threatened all the times. I have an older brother who is badly disabled. No one really cares. I know you talk about hope, but where is it? My boyfriend and his little brother and friend killed thimself. It will be 2 years ago tomarrow. I get abused and hurt so much, no one cares. People see the cuts, they see the bruises but no one cares. I try nd ask for help nd i get pushed away. Why should i be here. I wont to die. I have been raped and im scard to report it.

25

No one cares. Im cutting so much and doing such stupid stuff. Ill probably die. No one cares like, i try and ask, but no one cares. My dads emotionaly abusive, my moms an addict and physicaly abusive, her bf is a drunk and abusive, why should i [be] here? I wontto die. I know you dont care but yeah . . .

im Rachel, not that anyone cares.

Reggie's Initial E-mail Response to Rachel

Rachel, I need you to hear me: I do not want to push people away. I want to lead them to the place where they can find hope like I did. I know you have a purpose. I believe in you, even if you don't think so, okay?

Reggie

Rachel's Reply to Reggie's Response

???? you may say that now, but you wont care soon. You will wontto get rid of me too. You would wontto be the one to just push me away. Call me the weird person. I just cant do life. Ive cut so much over this youth rally. Its so pathetic i know. I never do this kind of stuff. Im so sorry i found your email. Im sorry im even writting this. I just dont know what to do anymore. I try. U really try but its *like why do i? I dont even know. I dont wont to be here anymore. I fractured 5 ribs the other month, got forced into . . . (message cut off)*

Reggie's Reply to Rachel

Dear Rachel,

Let me begin by saying something to you that someone should have said a long time ago—I am sorry. I know, I know—I am not the one who should be apologizing because I am not responsible for everything that has come your way. But please hear me when I say that on behalf of everyone who may never tell you what they should say, I, Reggie, am sorry for everything that has happened to you.

I'm sure you are not perfect, but you do not deserve all of this. I, Reggie, care about you. I know, this does not erase all that has happened to you, but do not underestimate the power of one person caring, one person loving. Yep, one person *can* change the world; I am counting on this to be true in you. Right now, *you* are *my* one person. But before that can happen, let me—the only person I can do anything about—change *your* world by loving you just the way you are.

You see, I really do believe in you, even if you don't think so. There is a purpose for you. If you really thought it was all over, you never would have written me. But you did write me. That means you are still breathing, and there is still hope. For

Rachel, there is still purpose. Who knows how your story might affect other people someday? Who knows if you might save someone's life?

Sometimes life is so difficult that it seems hard to breathe. Believe me, I've been there, and I know you are there right now. I know you want to give up, but you must not. Why? Because if you give up *today* in the middle of your problems, you will miss the very answer that is waiting for you right now in your *tomorrow*. It is there waiting for you. You just have to keep breathing long enough to reach it and take hold of it.

If you give up, you will become just another statistic, and no matter what the world says, no person is meant for this. If you were nothing but a statistic, your parents would have named you a number. Could you imagine being named *Seven* or *Twenty*? *Hey, Seven, quit counting stars and come to dinner!*

But, instead, you were given an actual name: Rachel. So you must keep breathing long enough to make that name great. I do not have all the answers, but I can tell you that I know what it is like to hurt deeply, to feel lost and abandoned, to consider ending my own life, to wonder if anyone cares. You are not alone in this. The path to survival is long and winding with many stops along the way, but it is a path *you can* walk. It is hard, but you are worth it.

So for now let me give you one answer you need to at least make it through today—no matter what, just keep breathing. These are not just empty words. This is not some motivational sports movie or just worthless inspiration. As long as you breathe, you live. As long as you are living, you can hope for tomorrow.

Remember that one large black man named Reggie thinks your name—Rachel—is already great. You are loved. So don't hate yourself. You can make it!

I Got Yo' Back!

Reggie Dabbs

Rachel's Reply to Reggie

I wonted to say that going to XX, I was going to not go. I was going to stay home and kill myself. I was going to take this razor i got and i was going to just let the blood go. But then i went to XX and was like i will just do it when i get home today. I was going to bleed to death like my boyfriend did. But you saved me. Last night. I had cut really bad. Should have goten stitches but it stoped bleeding this morning. i was siting in the bathroom just hurting because it was bleeding bad but then i got your email and i cryed so much.

LETTER 2:
IF I WAS MEANT TO LIVE, WHY THE H*** WOULD I WANT TO DIE?

"HANNAH"

Dear Reggie,

If I was meant to live, why the h*** would I want to die, huh? Can you tell me that, Reggie?

Hannah

Reggie's Reply to Hannah

Dear Hannah,

Yeah, I can tell you! I can tell you that the hurt and pain you are going through is so strong that you want to give up. It is a natural response to extreme hardship. When most people get really tired, they lay down to rest. When people get weak, they want to give up.

You feel like giving up is your only way out, but that is not true. I was right there in your shoes, and I wanted to give up too, but I held on because someday there was going to be someone like you who would have needed me to hold on. That's what separates us from everybody else. We won't give up; we won't lie down. There has to be a reason to hope.

You were not born just to be sixteen, and then just leave this world. There is something more for your life. So, yes, I can give you the answer—life. There is a reason we go through pain and sorrow. Life. Once we get through all that pain, there is love on the other side—contagious love that spreads to others. There is life on the other side of your pain.

I am writing you back because I have hope—hope that my own personal pain and sorrow in everything I have been through will somehow become hope for you too. No matter what you feel or how angry you are, I hope that you find hope because I answered your letter.

I had a guy ask me just today, "Why are you doing this? Why are you answering these letters? Nobody cares!" That's just it! If you *care* enough to write me the letter, then you should know that I *love* enough to answer. If you hurt enough to put these words on paper or in a Facebook "message" and send them, I will care enough to put my words on paper and send them back. What is this letter? It is a Band-Aid helping to heal your cut. It is a salve—like an ointment—to bring relief to wounds that may have been open too many years. It is hope for you when you have no hope, love when you have no love.

This letter is tomorrow in the middle of the pain you are facing today.

So why should you live? Because you are you—and there will never be another you. And we need you, even if you don't realize it yet. But the day will come when the world will need a hero, and because you have come through what you have come through, you will be the exact hero that we'll need tomorrow.

I Got Yo' Back!

Reggie Dabbs

LETTER 3:
I WILL NOT LET THE BULLIES WIN

"KAYLEE"

Dear Reggie,

My name is Kaylee, and you were at my high school in XX today. When I heard you were coming, I was so excited and kept telling all my friends, "Hey, I gotch yo back," and they started laughing and said, "I really can't wait for Reggie to brighten up my day." When you came to XX Middle School, I believe in 201X, I realized how much stronger I really was.

Freshman year was pretty rough, and I was trying to find my friend group and just went down a really bad path. I was bullied continuously. I battled depression for about 6 months. I told my mom that I had thoughts of hurting myself, and everything I kept bottled up inside finally exploded. That day was the hardest day but also the best day.

I started to see a therapist; that was my new best friend and favorite place to be. That room was a safe place for me to just pour out my feelings, and I only listened to him. I mean really listen; my mom and dad are the best parents in the world. I love them more than anything, but when you're stuck in a black whole with no light, you don't hear anything.

Fast forwarding a little, after all the times I saw my therapist, I got a lot better and was getting back to being myself. Those were the roughest 6 months I have ever gone through, and multiple times I had thoughts that if I just died tomorrow, no one would care and everyone would go on with their lives.

But I kept telling myself, I am strong, and I cannot and will not let those bullies win. They didn't win. Sorry for telling you everything about my past, but the whole reason why I am sending you this e-mail is to explain how I was one day going through my Facebook and saw you on my newsfeed. That day changed my life.

I looked at myself in the mirror and said, you can't let them win. Reggie didn't just come to your school for nothing; he came to tell you when one door closes, and even if that door shatters to bits and pieces when it closes, there's always another one waiting. Opened. Having you talk today really made me reflect on who I am as a person and come to the realization that I am strong.

I recently broke up with my boyfriend of 5 months

who was my best friend. I spent every day with him in the summer. He is a senior, and I am a sophomore, and I thought we are going to be dating for sure when he goes to college. But the feelings, the love I had for him, just vanished, and I tried so hard to find them, but they never came back. I am okay and know that if I could get through depression, I could get through this. I broke his heart, and I beat myself up every day for it.

But when you came today and told us about all the terrible, sad stories you have heard. That made me say to myself, "Keep your head high, and don't let anyone knock you down. You could someday make a difference in someone else's life and save them from something. You can do this, Kaylee."

Reggie, you're amazing; you made me the happiest I have been in 2 weeks, and for the time you were talking, all the thoughts about everything went away. All the stress was gone. I can't tell you how thankful I am for having you come today. When I reflect on today, I only remember me smiling and laughing.

I am thanking you from the bottom of my heart. And keep on doing what you do best, and that's changing people's lives. Thank you for taking your time today speaking and looking at this e-mail. Thank you, Reggie, and bless your heart, and wherever that great vibrant path you're on takes you, I bless it. You once again changed my life. Thank you.

Reggie's Reply to Kaylee

Dear Kaylee,

Thank you so much for believing in what I do! I love coming back to schools multiple times because I get to meet kids who saw me in middle school and then again in high school, just like you did.

I've heard that many kids who are teased and picked on never get over it. But I don't believe that has to be the case. Being bullied does not mean they can't go on to become great people. I have met many people who have been bullied or teased. Guys like NFL wide receiver DeSean Jackson, who said people made fun of him for being short. Just like you, he didn't let the bully keep him down. He decided to stand up for what is right. And I want you to know that I am proud of you. You were in the black hole. You said there was no light, but there is always light. There is always someone who will help you get to the other side. In your darkest night, in your toughest fight, someone is going to be there.

I'm glad I got to walk into your day, and I'm glad you remember me saying, "I Got Yo' Back!" That's why I say these words—people need to know that somebody is on their side. Even if I am out of sight, it doesn't mean I'm out of mind.

Love? Yeah, you're right. Sometimes when you love someone, it can really hurt. When I was reading this, I remembered one time when I was in middle school, I dated a cheerleader. Notice that I said one time. I took her to my favorite restaurant, which was also one I could afford: McDonald's.

Back then they had little squirt ketchup bottles. We went after a football game; she wanted some ketchup for her fries, and I offered to get it for her. I was trying to be a man and squeezed the bottle, but nothing would come out. She tried to help, but I insisted that I could do it. So I squeezed that bottle as hard as I could because I wanted to be a man. You can guess what happened. *Boom!* It exploded all over her cheerleading outfit. She jumped up, called me stupid, and walked out the door. I was depressed. I was in that black hole. But it didn't last long because I realized she had left food. So I ate her food and went home to watch *Happy Days*. (That's an old show from the 70s and 80s you should look up on Netflix.)

So everybody goes through that. And, yes, you are right. You are a princess, and your prince is going to come. Just keep getting up every day. Just keep living life. Helping people. Watching the sun rise. Just keep breathing. Everything will be all right, and you can make it, no matter what any bully says.

I Got Yo' Back!

Reggie Dabbs

EXHALE 1:
COULD ALL THIS BE TRUE?

When I asked a few younger friends to read over the first letter you just read, after some prodding, they reluctantly expressed a shared suspicion: there is no way Rachel's story can be completely true. It is just too much to happen to one person. Maybe she is making it up—piling it on for attention or dramatic effect?

This suspicion does not make them—or you, for that matter—horrible people for considering it. You are right. Rachel's story is extreme, and all of the letters to follow will not always deal with the lengthy laundry list of tragedies we see here. But we must face two crucial questions: Is her story true, and why is that an important question to ask?

You should know that Reggie actually met with Rachel, along with an adult close to her situation. Reggie saw the scars on her arms. He personally looked into her troubled eyes. He also spoke with the adult who confirmed the details of her story. So you see, Rachel's story may seem unbelievable, but the most unbelievable part is that it is definitely true.

When we hear stories like these, we want to either disbelieve them or simply wish them away. These are natural reactions. The details are just too much to process. In the age of social media and reality television, people often embellish their stories to gain attention. Sensationalism abounds.

We are so overstimulated with the crazy stories we hear on the news, in interviews, and on talk shows that we have become numb to them. The lands of reality and fiction have lost their borders, so we act as if the laws are the same in both places: *Just another person trying to get his fifteen minutes of fame. Just another crazy cartoon-type character to dismiss or ridicule. Man, what is wrong with people these days?*

But our suspicions often go too far. We stop seeing individuals and only see unlikely stories, to the point that we ignore the realities all around us. We see characters instead of people. These are just a few letters we have chosen out of thousands— thousands of stories with details similar to Rachel's. Abuse, rejection, bullying—they are not just buzzwords. People are really hurting and not just in cities where gangs are prevalent or poverty is high.

Right now, someone is being abused within the walls of a half-million-dollar home. Right now, someone is contemplating suicide in the middle of an advanced placement calculus class. Right now, someone in the building where you are reading this book is struggling with severe depression. Rachel's story may be extreme, but she represents what is really happening, and it is time for us to wake up and pay attention to the truth walking all around us.

Say these words out loud: *This really happened!* Now does Rachel have your attention? She definitely caught ours, which is why Reggie and I chose this letter to open the book. Suicide. Abuse. Hopelessness. The list goes on and on. As you can see, the issues this young woman faces seem both vast and unbearable. If you have a friend, a child, or a student who is facing situations like these, what can you possibly do for them? What can you say, or where can you go for help? Is there any hope?

Say these words out loud: *This really happened!* Now does Rachel have your attention?

First of all, you may need a little information that makes Rachel's letter as unique as each person who writes to Reggie. This letter is one of only a few in this book in which we will show you an actual conversation between Reggie and the writer. Most of the time, we will show you only a specific reply we are giving through this book, but this particular conversation happened in real time via e-mail, which Rachel references in her last message. Most of the letters to follow will simply be someone's story and our response to it; but in this case, we chose to also include Reggie's original response and Rachel's reactions to it.

Why is this important? Because we want you to come face-to-face with a harsh reality: after several heartfelt interactions, all of Rachel's problems are not resolved. Yes, we can see that Reggie's response made an impact, but note that Rachel's last message still finds her cutting and crying in the bathroom.

But the fact remains that even a gifted and caring person like Reggie did not fix Rachel's situation. Reggie Dabbs is by far the most effective communicator to students and adults in difficult situations I have ever met or even seen. What I mean is this: if he could not fix this, then you and I certainly will not do so either.

Great! Thanks so much for the encouragement. I thought this book was supposed to help us deal with these kinds of situations? Patience, my friend. In the pages to come we will offer many more specifics and takeaways, but to do so now would set us on the wrong course. The problems are not simple, so do not expect simple solutions. People in crisis do not need "just to be fixed." Their greater needs are to be listened to and valued.

Just take a gander at the huge laundry list of crises Rachel is facing: The suicide of close friends, which is leading her to similar thoughts for herself. A history of being sexually and emotionally abused and bullied. Obvious issues with depression. One of the faults of our modern age is to want a magic pill or a simple formula to—voilà!—make everything instantly okay. *Is there not a setting in my Facebook preferences that will make all of this go away?*

No, the answers are rarely simple, and seldom do they instantly make every negative issue go away. We have chosen this letter to open up the book because we actually want you to feel overwhelmed by where to start. Why?

It's reality: you cannot fix people. In fact, people will often quit listening to you if they think that is your only goal. Humans instinctively sense when you care more about getting *their* problem out of *your* way than actually caring about them.

Breathable Moment #1: People in crisis do not need "just to be fixed." Their greater needs are to be listened to and valued.

In the pages to come we will give you many concrete specifics about each of the critical issues addressed in this letter and more. But just as no one would build a house beginning with the attic, we begin with this foundation: caring about individuals, not just their problems. It may sound touchy-feely, and it may feel as if it does no good since simply caring today does not necessarily produce a completely different set of circumstances tomorrow. But that is the point. If we care, then we will invest ourselves in the lives of others past the point of just tomorrow. We will invest for years—for life.

So sometimes the goal is simply to get them to their tomorrow, even if it appears their tomorrow will not look much different than their today. You cannot fake concern, nor should you. If you want to help, you must start by truly caring, even if people seem broken beyond any hope of repair. *Your* compassion is the first plank in building the bridge of *their* hope. If you care, then there is hope.

When Reggie and I discussed this particular letter, he was

adamant about letting people know that Rachel is a great example of how important it is for friends, parents, and teachers to listen and respond when people cry out for help, either vocally or silently. These are pivotal moments that can easily be missed.

You never know how meaningful your smile or your random *hello* might be. People in crisis are not always wearing it on their sleeves. They may be your own children, and it is crucial that beyond today's issues they know that you love them. So tell them constantly and never assume they will just know it on their own. They may be a stranger. Again, become a caring person, and you will become a part of the answer.

We do not have to get a response every time we show people that we care; we *just do it* because we actually *just care*. We do not always know where they are on the inside. They may be in the bathroom bleeding. They may be holding the loaded gun. They may be living to die instead of dying to live.

If we care, then we will invest ourselves in the lives of others past the point of just tomorrow.

We must do our best to answer. We must reach out. Even though it hurts and though we may be hurting too, we have to help others keep breathing another day. Again, we do not do this just to fix them; we do this because we actually care. Yes, there will be improvement in their situations, and we will keep discussing ways that can happen, but we must begin here.

And in Rachel's case, if Reggie had not cared enough to listen, her breath would have stopped forever. There are people out there just waiting for you to care. Your caring might keep them breathing another day.

SIGNATURE 1:
LEAVE YOUR OWN IMPRESSION

1. What were your initial emotional reactions to Rachel's letter? What did they reveal about your perception of people in crisis?

2. Have you known anyone who has had similar experiences to Rachel's? Explain.

3. Before reading Reggie's and John's thoughts, how might you have tried to fix the situation? Why do you think that is your first reaction in moments like this?

4. Do you think people can tell when you care more about "getting *their* problem out of *your* way than actually caring about them"? Can you tell?

5. Can you name someone who cared about you more than fixing your problem? How did this affect your life?

Notes

_____

_____

_____

_____

_____

_____

Roles and Holes

LETTER 4:
YOU SAVED MY LIFE, DAD!

"LAUREN"

Dear Reggie,

I know you're a very busy person and if you don't get to respond to me then i understand, I just want you to know how much you helped me. You came to XX school Friday, november X, 201X. I can't thank you enough. We've had multiple students commit suicide within the last year. Students, children, friends. We needed you Reggie, I needed you. You told us your story, Now I want to tell you mine.

In the fourth row, head phones in, eyes closed, ready to ignore another "stupid, pointless assembly", there I was. I'm a junior and Friday morning, I was ready to say goodbye. Tired of being called names. Being told i'm useless, worthless. A lot of times it's common words, fat-ugly-slut-etc. I guess people are too ignorant to realize those words hurt worse than being punched in the gut and kicked while you're down. It all lead to cutting, and wishing to be gone. I didn't want anyone to know, I didn't want any help. I thought everyone was going to laugh at me and say it was stupid to do. Maybe it is. Who knows?

But it really helps to lessen the pain I feel inside. If I feel the cuts and see blood run, it's a temporary high. It gives me something a little more bearable to focus on. I don't want you to think i'm just another dumb teenager looking for attention. That's not it at all. I try my best to stay out of the spotlight. Blending my way through things, releasing stress by self-harm. I guess what i'm trying to say is please don't just chalk me up as an, excuse the expression, attention whore.

Within the first 5 minutes of you talking, I turned down my music. A few minutes later I took out the headphones all together and started listening. I felt like you were only talking to me. And it wasn't like you were judging me, that's what most people do. Nobody likes me. Not even my father. He hates me most of all. I don't know what I did to him. I guess i just wasn't good enough. He left when I was little. I'm sixteen now. I don't need him, I have enough people that put me down. He called a few months ago, don't know how he got my number, said he wanted to meet and talk. Of course, i said yes. Maybe he really did love me.

I've never been so wrong in my life. He wanted me to sign papers saying that he didn't have to claim me as his kid. That there would no longer be any ties, legally or anything else. So I said screw it, i'm done. I'm tired of trying to get people to accept me. I'm done trying to fit in. I don't want it. I don't need it. The only thing i need is my razor. It's worked for a long time, it won't fail me now. And if it did, would i care? No.

I'm done talking about my past, you don't want to know. I know there is people who have it a lot worse than i do. But just know that there are so many things that i didn't tell you. I've been through a lot of s***. It's been a rough life, and i'm not even half way through. Two of my friends recently decided they were done. They're gone. I'm alone. Why can't I go too? It was so easy for them! It could be like that for me too. Whatever, look, I think that i'm always going to be looking for a way out. That's just something i can't help, and nobody else wants to help.

But when I get down that low, I think of your poem. It means a lot to me because i write poetry too. I wrote yours down, i carry it with me. That way if i get that depressed again, which happens way too often, then i can read it. I remember that you sounded really sincere. You don't have to know my name to know my pain, you have your own. I believe that. When you were talking I felt like you knew me for a long time, like you knew every mistake i've ever made and every bad thing that's happened to me.

And for the first time, it felt like someone actually cared what happened to me. You love me when you don't even know me. You love me when I hate myself, and everyone else does too. You love me when i'm alone, every day of my life. Thank you so much for making me stop and think for a minute. Because to be honest with you, I was planning on leaving everything behind. When i woke up friday morning, i decided that i was done. And friday after school, nobody was going to have to deal with me anymore. Everyone could be happy with me gone. But now i know that you would care, somehow you would know. And you would be disappointed in me. I don't want to disappoint you.

I'm trying my hardest to hold on, it's not easy. But i'll do my best. Thanks for loving me when no one else was there. Thank you for saving my life, even if only temporarily.

I'll never forget you, Dad.

Reggie's Reply to Lauren

Dear Lauren,

You said that you carry *my* poem with you, but I want to let you know that for a long time now, I have been carrying *your* letter in my bag everywhere I go. It reminds me why I get up in the morning. Why I constantly leave my wife to travel. Why I have missed some of my son's birthdays. Ball games. Anniversaries. Why I fly all around this world. It reminds me why I am trying to lose weight so I can stay on this planet just a little bit longer.

Your letter reminds me of how I was able to get through my own pain and sorrow. I know what it is like to be called dumb, and I want you to know that you are not dumb. I would never chalk you up as just another statistic. I want you to know that I do care.

You see, I know that somehow, some way, all that hurt you are going through is going to help you reach someone else in the same way I reached you. Someday you will write a poem, and others are going to take off their headphones and read it. They are going to tattoo it on their arms because your words have changed their lives. Your words have already changed mine.

Someday, you will be a parent yourself. Somewhere, somehow the hurt you are going through with your own father and mother will produce this result in your life: your own kids will never feel the hurt you are going through. Someday your pain will actually make a difference in the lives of your children.

I am answering your letter because, deep down inside, I don't want anyone to have to grow up the way you have had to. We don't want anybody to have to hurt the way we hurt. We want to do our part to be *the answer* for someone.

But the crazy part about you, Lauren, is that *you* are a part of *my answer*. Your pain, your sorrow, and the rejection from your father make you a huge part of my answer. I get up every day knowing I'll get to meet you again—and other people dealing with similar situations. Knowing that you will write my poem down again. Knowing that maybe you'll write me again, asking me to not call you names or call you dumb—which I would never do. Knowing that even though you have faced so much, you really do care about me.

Every day I wake knowing that at the end of your letter, you have given me the greatest honor of calling me Dad. As your dad, I think the world of you. I know you're going to make it. That is why I do this. Because I carry your letter and hope for you making it in my bag everywhere I go.

You are why I do this.

I Got Yo' Back!

Reggie Dabbs

LETTER 5:
MY DAD DIED, AND I BLAMED MYSELF

"MADISON"

Dear Reggie,

Hello, I'm Madison. I was the girl that came up to you with the black hat.

My story. My father passed away when I was three. For years upon years, when I understood what happened to him, I blamed myself. And since the day I understod, I have had this hole in my heart . . . and I have tried everything to fill it. Today, I am a 15 year old teen, confused, scared, and lost.

Throughout my life i have been beaten by foster parents, by family's boyfriends, by people I don't even know. I grew up in pure hell and torture. I lost my mom for 5 years due to her love for alcohol and not her own kids.

I have been bullied and sexually harassed.

I have been kidnapped and raped.

I have self-harmed before.

I am more then ashamed with myself. But I still have this hole in my heart, and its huge.

Today when you said "I am a father to the fatherless" a door opened, opportunity . . . I felt for once I had someone to go to and I really do hope you reply it'd mean everything to me. I just need a little help. I have been way too strong for way too long. I'm ready to give way. I just need someone to talk to. I don't wanna end my life. But I feel like I just wanna shut down, AND shut every one away . . . help . . .

Reggie's Reply to Madison

Dear Madison,

The very last word you wrote is what sticks out the most in my mind and my heart: *help*. I'd love to.

That's why I came to your school. When I go to so many schools, I see hundreds of thousands of faces, but sometimes it seems that I only get to reach a few hearts. I put up with the hundreds of thousands of faces because I know that behind every face is a heart—a chance. Many of those kids have holes in their hearts.

I don't know the first thing about medicine, but a person I met told me I was one of the greatest surgeons in the world because I do heart surgery—that I help people fill the holes in their hearts. I do not think I am great at this, but I can say that over the past twenty years, I have tried to fill those holes with one word: *love*. As an injured patient in this life myself, I know what love can do.

You said you were ashamed of yourself. I know some things happen in life that are our fault, and some things happen that are someone else's fault. Many people do not know that both can cause us shame.

You feel shame, and most of it is not your fault. It's not your fault that your dad died. It's not your fault you were abused. It's not your fault, okay?

If you will believe me when I say it is not your fault, then you can also believe the next thing I really want to tell you: I think you are awesome! I think eventually the world is going to see you shine because you are going to make it. I know your past is horrible, but I am here to tell you what I tell so many: your past is your history, but your future is your destiny. These are not empty words—they are really true.

You have had tragedies, but your life does not have to be a tragedy. It can become a trophy. It can let the world see what happened in your past and how you have survived. You can help other people who are deeply hurt because you really know what it means to hurt deeply.

You are not alone. Other people have holes in their hearts too—including me. But I am still breathing. Why? Because I did something that can be very hard to do. I let somebody love me. It sounds so simple, but it can be so hard to reach out, so hard to let love in. You may not know me that well, but please know that I offer to you the love that you deserve. Will you take it?

My mind goes back to a fairy tale about a little princess named Snow White. Everyone thought she was dead, but the prince still loved her enough to offer her the kiss of love to bring her back again. Evil said that if she was dead, nobody would care anymore. If she was gone, no one would reach out to her ever again.

But love says, "You are worth another chance. I will reach out one more time." I know you have a hole in your heart, but don't give up. If you are ashamed of yourself or your past, don't give up. Love is the prince, and you are still Snow White even if everyone thinks you are dead—including you.

Hold on for just one more kiss, just one more breath, just one more day because tomorrow will be the answer to the problems you have today. I know you are going to make it. Just keep reaching out because someone is going to reach in and help you with your broken heart. You are not alone. You are not unloved.

I Got Yo' Back!

Reggie Dabbs

But love says, "You are worth another chance. I will reach out one more time."

LETTER 6:
I WILL BE GREAT!

"BRIANNA"

Dear Reggie,

You've officially made me your daughter yesterday. February XX, 200X. I will forever be thankful for that day. Even though [it] was just a few seconds of you speaking directly to me and no one else, I felt your love. That is a God sent gift.

I haven't come from the best of situations either. I was and still am the protector in my family. I have the ownership and the burden of protecting my mother and my younger brother. You are also a protector, but you protect others in a different way than I do. You protect others with words, feelings, and love. It felt good to be protected, instead of being the protector.

It is because of God sent people like you that will help millions, if just for one day, appreciate, cherish,

and make it in this world and through their daily lives.
I want to be a great protector like you. Throughout my
life I have wanted nothing more but to help people of
all ages as you do. I have always been the one to push
myself to do better in my situation, to look on the
good side of things, and to help anyone that would let
me. It felt good to hear someone else telling me that I
can do it. That I can be successful in my life despite my
situations in my life. That life is only what you make
it. And being one of your many daughters, I love you so
much for that.

You now being the dad I never had to push me a little
further to be the best I can, and to protect me, I will do the
best I can and I will be successful. You are truly a blessing.
I love you very much and I thank God for you. And I thank
you for what you have done for me.

Sincerely,

Your Daughter, Brianna

P.S. I have always wanted to be a daddy's girl!

Reggie's Reply to Brianna

Dear Brianna,

I love the way you say in your letter, "I want to be . . . I can
be . . . I will be." But actually, I'm going to have to change that to

something more accurate: you are. You are great right now. You are a champion now. To me, you are a legend.

I tell kids all the time in schools that there are two kinds of people in the world: you are either a part of the problem, or you are part of the answer. Brianna, you are the answer, and I'm very very proud of you! To protect your mom and your little brother the way you do, you are the answer. To write to a guy like me and give me hope in the middle of my hectic, crazy day of doing schools, you are the answer. I'm sure on the bus, in the car, and walking down the sidewalk you smile at people, and you are their answer.

Your words to me today reminded me that even when we don't feel like it, we still protect, and we still love. You reminded me that you still give. I'm proud of you. And I am honored and more proud than ever to say, "Yeah, you're my daughter!" It's with a lot of distance, and I know that in some ways, it is only in words, but still, I am so proud to say it.

Since you are my daughter, I want you to know that I love you. And though you are great already, you are still going to become even greater. You are right: you *are* going to change the world, and I will be watching and cheering for you as you do it.

I Got Yo' Back!

Reggie Dabbs

EXHALE 2:
SPOONS AND SHOVELS

I will never forget the moment Reggie told me that he carries Lauren's letter with him. Honestly, I was floored, not because I would not expect Reggie to do things like that but more so because he deals with so many incredibly difficult situations like this that I cannot fathom how he keeps up.

So every time I read a letter to Reggie from one of the millions of people he speaks to every year, and he says, "Oh yeah, I remember her," I am reminded why he is such a special voice to this generation. He is the best example I know of what we talked about in the first letter: he cares first and fixes second. He is also an example of what each of us can be if we will care enough to listen and respond.

Once again, these letters are filled with a host of difficult issues to face, so let us simply examine how you can help and not inadvertently do more damage when you face something similar in your own life or relationships. How can you help?

I wish you could read the thousands of Facebook "messages,"

e-mails, and letters that come to Reggie. You would be astounded at the vast number of girls like Brianna who address him as Dad or Daddy. They call him by this title because during his school presentations, he shares his own painful story about growing up in foster care and feeling abandoned by his biological father, whom to this day he still has never met.

Since Reggie never knew his real father, he tells crowds about his adopted parents—his biological mom's English teacher and her husband, the school janitor—who showed him what real love and acceptance are all about. Reggie then goes on to tell all who will listen that if they feel abandoned by the adults in their lives, he will do what was once done for him: he will gladly take on the honor of being their daddy.

Fatherlessness and a general overwhelming feeling of parental abandonment or neglect is more than just a recurring theme in the letters we receive. Fatherlessness is usually the central core of the whole matter. And the way Reggie deals with this issue, as we see in this letter, is extreme, to say the least.

You may be a teacher reading this book, thinking to yourself, *I can't tell my students that I'll be their mommy or daddy! I'll go to jail! Besides, don't they need me to remain an authority figure more than a friend?*

Or maybe you are one of those "terrible" parents that students write to Reggie about—and you know the other side of the story that your teen is either leaving out or cannot see from his adolescent perspective. Maybe you have made some huge mistakes, maybe not. Either way, if you are reading this book, you are probably trying to see some things improve, and no matter what kind of parent you are, I doubt that you like the idea of your kid calling another guy Daddy.

Or maybe you are just a friend dealing with a peer—someone your own age. How does Reggie's practice of calling himself someone's daddy help you at all?

Fatherlessness is usually the central core of the whole matter.

Besides all of these questions, is it even a good thing for Reggie to be so emotionally forward with strangers? Is he not giving students an inappropriate moment of false hope since he cannot be their real daddy? No matter what he calls himself, he cannot go home with millions of people and be the father they never had, and neither can you or I.

To address all of these, we must clarify a few things about Reggie's approach. First of all, he is very clear to students and adults alike that his willingness to be called their daddy is not, and obviously cannot be, literal. He blatantly tells them that he cannot *actually* go home with them and fix all their problems. Rather his aim is for a broader target: their hearts.

He does not fill a *role*; he fills a *hole*. In other words, he offers them what he has to give: genuine concern and love. These may not seem like much on the surface; rather they are like first responders to the scene of the disasters that have inflicted the deep wounds you are reading about here. Reggie responds even though the disastrous situations themselves are usually beyond his abilities to change.

Yes, he will have to board a plane and go to the next town, the next school, and the next group of students. However, the people who write these letters to their daddy, Reggie, seem to have no delusions otherwise. They are not waiting up for him at night to come home or asking him for a weekly allowance.

They know Reggie cannot literally fill the *role* of daddy, yet they have no problem assigning him this title after only hearing him for forty-five minutes. That is crazy, right? Maybe not. It is amazing what forty-five minutes of real, genuine concern can do in someone's life, even if Reggie is not the speaker.

Reggie's genuine care and communication does not take away their situation, but it does begin to add small shovelfuls of emotional fill dirt back into the gaping craters of their wounded hearts. They may need truckloads, but even a shovelful offered in a short school assembly can make a difference. By addressing their daddy issues directly instead of dancing around them, as well as opening up to them about his own similar pain, Reggie offers them *hope* even if he cannot offer them a *home*. Besides, for many people, hope is a safer place than their real homes.

Since their situations may be the same when they go home from the assembly, is Reggie shoveling false hope? We think not. Hope is hope. It has substance even if it comes from a stranger, even if nothing immediately changes. A kind word makes a difference. One person extending love to another can plant a seed of hope that might lay dormant for years yet still blossom someday.

Now back to you. Maybe you have felt ineffective with your friends, students, children, or even parents because you have not possessed the ability to fill the huge role they obviously need filled. Let us empower you with this truth: you do not have to completely fill every crevice of crisis to make a difference. If Reggie can offer hope in a forty-five minute presentation, just imagine what you can do living day in and day out near those who need hope? For you, it may only start with a spoonful, but let it start.

You cannot always fill *roles*, but you can always fill *holes*. I do not mean you can completely fill the void, but you can toss what love, concern, and positive outlook you do have into what may seem like an abyss of hopelessness. You never know what it might do in the long run. Never let the fear of making false promises inadvertently keep you from making any kind of promises. Make promises you *can* keep. You can promise to care, love, and listen. When you have nothing to offer, you can still offer hope.

Honestly, we do not suggest doing what Reggie does by offering yourself to be called Daddy or something else similar. This may very well not work for you in your situation. You must take into account that Reggie's unparalleled ability to communicate verbally, his own personal tragic story, and his two decades of influence globally all combine for a very unique moment in the lives of those who hear him speak.

Breathable Moment #2: You cannot always
fill *roles*, but you can always fill *holes*.

You must find your own unique way to help. But above all
else, do not be afraid to offer hope to someone whose situation seems hopeless. You do not have to be Reggie to offer help
and hope.

As an educator, you can remain in control of your classroom yet still offer some level of humanity to your students,
reflecting that you actually see more than just their academic or
behavioral angst. You can be a decent human in the midst of an
often indecent, unreasonable classroom environment. You, not
the content you teach, can add a shovelful of hope.

Never let the fear of making false promises inadvertently keep you from making any kind of promises.

As a parent, you can continue to face what seems to be an
impossible uphill climb: constant change and constant conflict.
But even amidst the madness of family, you can speak hope or,
perhaps, stop speaking words that are the opposite of hope. You
can add another shovelful into the gaping hole.

As a friend, you do not have to fix them, but you can hold
out for hope when they want to give up. You can keep pointing

out what is coming tomorrow—another day. Hope itself, apart from the unpredictable details of how things change or do not change, could be the only thing that keeps them breathing.

Sometimes, hope for another day's breath is the best help we can offer.

SIGNATURE 2:
LEAVE YOUR OWN IMPRESSION

1. Why do you think people instinctively want to share their own stories with Reggie when they hear his tragic story?

2. What were your thoughts when you read that Reggie carries Lauren's letter with him wherever he goes?

3. Why might people be hesitant to offer hope to someone like Lauren or Madison? What are we afraid of?

4. What qualifications are required for offering hope? How is it something anyone can do? How do Brianna's words offer you hope?

5. Can you think of people in your life who need a spoonful of your hope to begin filling holes? Perhaps you have not seen them in this way because you know you cannot fill the role they need filled.

Notes

_____

_____

_____

_____

_____

_____

CHAPTER 3

Bullies and Backstories

LETTER 7:
I JOINED A GANG, AND NOW THEY WANT TO KILL ME!

"CARLOS"

Dear Reggie,

My name is Carlos, and you came to X High School today! I was one of the people that had to stand up. I wanted to write to you and tell you how much your story and your presentation impacted me today. I was trying to hold back the tears because that was me. I was the one being bullied. Here's my story, and I hope you share this one day.

When I was younger, I was constantly harassed and bullied as a child, and the constant torture led me to make a life-altering desicion. When I turned 12 years old, I was initiated into a gang. A powerful notorious gang called the Latin Kings. I only joined to feel accepted and to stop my tormentors. I'm 18 now and did and

seen things people can't imagine. I don't know if you're
religious, but I recently started going to church and
learned about the message you were trying to get across.
and that's love!

Bullying destroyed my life beyond repair. I decided I
don't want to be a gang member anymore. I quit about
2 weeks ago, but if you know anything about gangs, it's
blood in blood out! They are looking for me and want to
kill me, but I guess it's what I deserve, right? People look
at me like I'm the scum of society, but even a cold hard
gang member has a story of hurt and a dark past! Not all
of us are lost causes. I'm sad I couldn't make my short
breath of life count for something because that's what
life is, a short breath, a vapor that disappears!

I know I don't have long to live because I can't walk
out my house without fear, but I accepted my fate today.
I just wish someone like you could have talked to me when
I was younger. God bless you. Reggie, I want you to tell my
story, and maybe you could prevent a kid from joining
a gang and ruining his life like I did! I never wanted
this life, and I wish I could change it all! I'm sad but not
for myself. I caused this. But I'm sad for the child that
me and my girlfriend are expecting. I probably won't
be around for his or her birth, and it kills me inside.
Another child growing up without a father. I don't want
my child to know me as "Carlos the gang member," but I
guess I can't help that!

I hope God loves me enough to save my soul because I belong in hell . . . but I saw how love can change a person and change the world. You proved to me that there is love. There is forgiveness. There is love in times of need, and when life is cold, there is a promise! Love is changing my life. I just wish I could be around longer and see my child grow up!

Don't quit on any child, Reggie, even a cold hearted gang member because even they are people with a lot of hurt! Thank you for what you do and thank you for visiting. You're a blessing. I wish I could see you again!

Carlos

Reggie's Reply to Carlos

Dear Carlos,

First of all, no man knows when his time is over. No man knows when he will breathe his last breath. Even if there is a hit out on your life, do not throw in the towel as if your life is over. Live every day the best you can.

Remember, too, that your past is your history, but your future is your destiny. There is a way to get to your future. You have chosen to do right today, and that is something you will be able to live with tomorrow. I believe you will see your child, you will grow up, and you will become something great.

You speak with regret about the things you have done and

rightly so, but listen, my friend, *your* story is *your* story. And I believe your story is not over. I believe *you* will be able to tell it. In my mind's eye, I see you at assembly programs speaking about how you made it out of a gang and changed your life. And what you thought was all bad changed to something incredibly good.

I believe that young people will write you and say, "Thank you for sharing your story. Thank you for making it through the hurt." I believe that someday you'll be me, but more effective. You'll be answering letters like this. Telling people that there is hope—that even when we make mistakes, there is still hope. The past you know is your past, but the future you do not yet know is your destiny.

Do not forget that somebody is going to be there for you. Find an adult to talk to from school or church—anywhere. Never give up because you are not alone. Never alone. Never hopeless.

I Got Yo' Back!

Reggie Dabbs

LETTER 8:
TWO TEENS IN AUSTRALIA HAVE JUMPED IN FRONT OF TRAINS . . . HELP!

"KAYLA"

Dear Reggie,

Australia needs your help. In this past week alone two young teens have committed suicide by jumping in front of trains. I have a lot of friends who are depressed, and I don't want them to be next. Can you please come and share your story? These kids are being bullied to death, and I know that you would have a great impact on teens' lives if you came and spoke here.

Hopefully you can help.

Kayla

XX, Australia

Reggie's Reply to Kayla

Dear Kayla,

Four words rang out in my mind when I read your letter: *I am so desperate!* That some kids are so desperate they would jump in front of trains to kill themselves—that is desperate. But you have to understand if there are kids who are that desperate, hope is also available. I'm so sorry you lost your friends like that, but there is always someone near you who can speak hope to your other friends—and to you.

Don't give up! This is why we started coming to Australia seventeen years ago, and we will continue to come to Australia. We'll never stop coming there because everybody needs hope. I wish I could clone myself and speak more places and more times, but that is why we partner with so many organizations and with all the speakers and resources they are providing. We do this so we can go to more places and reach more people.

So hang in there because we're coming. We're going to help you and your friends. But for now, *you* can be there for your friends. Ask them the hard questions. When they are quiet in class, ask them if they're okay. Be willing to step out and put yourself out there because one day the answer is going to be no, and you are going to be able to help them. Always be watching so you can always be ready to help your friends.

I Got Yo' Back!
Reggie Dabbs

LETTER 9:
HOW DO I ERASE THE NAMES: WHORE, LESBIAN, POTHEAD, ALCOHOLIC?

"ALEXIS"

Dear Reggie,

First off I hope I didn't get the rong e-mail. . . . But anywho . . . u r the 1st person to semi relate to me . . . I remember every yr wen I was a lil girl my mom would ask me wat I wanted for Christmas and I would always tell her my dad, not knowin how bad it hurt her . . . And everywhere I went I'd look for him . . . I'm a month shy from 18 and I met my dad for the 1st time in april . . . It was better not to know him . . . U spoke of ur mom dying of cancer well my uncle is dying having a couple weeks left to live. . . . I spent my whole Christmas break taking my aunt to radiation every day . . . She is in her 60s and well we r just hopin for 1 more year w/ her. . . . My life has become not mine anymore . . . I met u 2 yrs ago at XX and u moved me . . . All I could think was how much better our school would b if we had someone like u to motivate others. . . . But how do I erase the name "whore" "lesbian" "pothead" "alcoholic" . . . I have made sum horrible mistakes and I cant even sit in a class without hating who i am . . . My [boyfriend is] not the same color as me, the kid w/ "XX" shaved in his head lol, and that just makes me judged more . . . I just don't understand who I am anymore. . . . do u?

Please help me . . .

Reggie's Reply to Alexis

Dear Alexis,

There are two types of people in the world. Listen carefully. There are people who are part of the problem, and people who are part of the answer. I need you to be a part of the answer. You know what it is like to be called these horrible words, these names. Now you know what people in the world feel like who think they can't make it or handle it anymore. But because you know that pain, I believe hurting people can help hurting people.

Number one, I need you to understand that you are not the words people call you. You are not without value. When people say you are nothing or useless, you are worth more than that.

Number two, I need you to understand that there is a plan for every breathing human being on this planet. The only way for you to live up to that plan is to make a choice. My choice is my choice too.

Number three, most of all, you need to understand that someone is always going to love you just the way you are. Never ever give up. Keep breathing. Keep walking. Keep moving. And when you get depressed and lonely, let someone walk with you. It's hard to walk alone. Sometimes you need somebody stronger to help carry you. Today it was me. But there is always someone. Don't believe the things people say that bring you down. Believe instead in the hope that people bring to you.

I Got Yo' Back!

Reggie Dabbs

EXHALE 3:
BULLY BACKSTORIES

These three letters are as different as night and day, yet they share a common thread: bullying. We hear about bullying all over the news, in assemblies at school, and even at home around the dinner table with our families.

For many of us who are older, what some call *bullying* today was just called *life* when we were kids. Getting picked on. Wedgied. Teased. Once again, it is always a temptation to dismiss letters like these because it seems so many people are crying bully that it cannot all be true.

Yes, we think there is definitely a need for people to not immediately cry bully every time they face difficulty in life, even if it is from a person. Some of this is simply the way the world is, even if it is not ideal. If you haven't yet discovered it for yourself, the world is not always a nice place.

We are not saying to just accept the negativity or that bullying should ever be tolerated. We just know that people do have the ability to rise above the negativity of the world by their attitudes and choices, even if they cannot necessarily change the negativity by doing so. You cannot control how much you live in this ugly world, but you can control how much of this ugly world lives in you.

Helping people rise above a victim mentality is one of our main goals, but the truth still remains that many people out there are being legitimately victimized by extreme or excessive bullying. At an alarming rate, students are harming themselves, harming others, and even killing themselves over this issue. Like it or not, we must work to reverse these trends.

Our friends at the Youth Alliance state that every school day 160,000 students in the United States miss school for fear of being bullied. All told, 32 percent of students between the ages of twelve and eighteen report being bullied each year.[1]

You cannot control how much you live in this ugly world, but you can control how much of this ugly world lives in you.

How do we distinguish between what is normal teenage mischief and what is dangerous or inappropriate? When does messing around go too far to the point that people become messed up? And how could this issue be so powerful that people would rather jump in front of speeding trains than deal with what they are facing at school?

As Reggie points out, many people who feel bullied are obviously beyond the point of desperation. Carlos's letter shows us what often happens when people are pushed too far—they become the very thing they hate. In Carlos's case he joined a gang to get away from his tormentors, and thus he became one of the tormentors himself.

Though there is not a cut-and-dry answer that always tells us when innocent joking becomes harmful bullying, there are a few ways to detect when things are going too far, as they did for Carlos. Here are a few telltale signs:

- If someone is threatened, injured, or experiencing damage to his or her property.
- If someone is being teased to the point of insult, ridicule, or humiliation.
- If someone is rejected, excluded, isolated, or treated as inferior.

When is the line crossed into the land of bullying? We think it is when people no longer think it is funny. If they do not feel like they are in on the joke, then things are beginning to go too far. When the joke excludes or isolates them instead of includes them. And obviously, if and when someone is threatening or doing them physical harm, the line has long since been crossed.

This kind of treatment is what transformed Carlos from a

victim into a bully. Yes, it can happen that quickly. The "if you can't beat them, join them" mind-set is more common than you might think. People will walk down very dark paths if they think the darkness will hide the target on their backs.

Carlos may not have jumped in front of a moving train, like those tragically desperate kids in Australia, but he did lay down on his own set of tracks to get away from the pain. He tried to throw his life so far away that the bullies could not find it.

But the problem is not just *a* person. It is not just *a* bully. Yes, each person is solely responsible for his or her actions; no one is trying to debate that fact. But a bigger problem lies in people as a whole—and the fact that much of the time, the whole of society approves of what is happening by saying or doing nothing to stop it. Society is allowing this—a society of people.

You cannot escape people. Not by laying low. Not by joining a gang. Not by moving to Antarctica. Trying to escape people while living in this world is like trying to escape water while swimming—it is just not possible. The answer is not to escape from or eliminate all bullies. In fact, we believe that at least part of the answer actually lies within the problem itself: people.

Every bully has a backstory. Some people who lash out at others are either subconsciously or purposefully doing what they feel is necessary to address their own desperate situations, backgrounds, or experiences. Others lash out for none of these reasons. They engage in bullying not out of a reaction to any crisis in their own lives but simply because doing so is easy for them. It may be reflective of how they are currently wired emotionally.

This does not mean they cannot grow past this behavior, but research shows that the idea that all bullies are insecure, have low self-esteem, or are overcompensating for something else done to them is simply not true. Yes, Carlos may have engaged in bullying behavior to escape his own bullying situation, but this is not the case for all bullies. It has been shown that bullies generally do not have low self-esteem but rather a low degree of empathy. They may actually feel great about themselves, but they do not necessarily internalize how the consequences of their actions adversely affect those whom they bully or themselves.[2]

So sometimes a bully's background is the main component of his backstory. But other times, a bully's brain is the main component. Sometimes people just make poor choices for seemingly no reason at all. Regardless, you can take note of their backstories—even if the main storyline is that they lack a healthy level of empathy—and begin to value them.

When you read Carlos's letter in this book, you probably feel like we do: proud of him. Hopeful for his breath to continue. Glad that he has seen the light and accepted change into his life. But if you had encountered him in the middle of his violent gang years, he likely would have been to you nothing but a nameless, faceless, and worthless gang member—some guy you instinctively move away from when you walk down the street.

He would have been the bully. The monster. The problem. The reason other people jump in front of trains. Unreachable. Unworthy of love.

Breathable Moment #3: Every bully has a backstory.

The bully himself is the most obvious villain for all of us to unite against. And, yes, we do believe in standing up to bullies and defending ourselves or those around us who need help. But the problem is not as simple as: some people are heroes, and others are villains. On any given day you know that you can be either one; people are not completely defined by their best or worst moments. No one is always a hero, and we believe those nasty bullies out there are not always villains, even if they rarely show it. Like Carlos, we believe they can someday still become heroes. We must not unite against bullies but against bullying itself.

Carlos started down the path he chose because he himself was bullied, not because he wanted to become a bully. Sure, there are people out there who do not have tragedy as the backdrop of their bad choices—they just seem to make bad choices. But even when it is not tragedy, there is always still a backstory. Insecurity. Inferiority issues. A need for approval at the expense of others. Or as we said, just a general lack of empathy or understanding of the severity of consequences. Dig deep enough; you'll find it.

In the letters and exhales to come, we will continue to give more concrete tips for what to do when you are either being bullied, are tempted to do the bullying, or are bullying someone already and do not realize the severity of your actions. For now, we want to help you see the problem as broad as it really is.

It is not just about a bully or a kid being picked on. It is about all of us. We must all address it, or it will never go away. We hope this book will empower you not just to view the problem from a distance but also to see your role in it. Your need to see it happening and take appropriate actions to intervene. Your ability to save a life from destruction because you understand the power of positive and negative words.

Every bully and every victim may not read these words, but you are reading them right now. Just like Neo from the movie *The Matrix*, you can take one of two pills. The blue one will allow you to continue living in your own little reality that is not really reality at all. It is a place where bullies and victims both are like movie characters that entertain you or move you to pity. But they never move you to action.

Or you can take the red pill and wake up! You can see the world for what it really is. You can see those students in your class as more than just whiners. You can see their backstories and begin to value them. Protect them. You can see those bullies, gang members, mean gossipers, and troublemakers as products of some untold backstories too.

You can become a part of the solution even if you have never considered yourself a part of the problem. As we will soon see, we are each a part of one or the other.

SIGNATURE 3:
LEAVE YOUR OWN IMPRESSION

1. When you read the letter from Carlos, were your first reactions sympathetic or harsh? Why do you think you felt this way?

2. If you are honest with yourself, before reading Kayla's letter, did you consider the problem of bullying to be as extreme as in her letter? Would you have thought someone would jump in front of a train over it?

3. Where do you think the line is between innocent playfulness among friends and harmful bullying? Do you know someone who has been bullied or called names as Alexis was?

4. In what ways is bullying worse in our modern culture than in times past due to technology, social media, and so forth? Have you ever read something derogatory or hateful on someone's Facebook "page" or Twitter feed?

5. How can it be easy to dismiss the bullies themselves as the sole cause of this issue in the world? Though they are definitely responsible for their own actions, how does each person's backstory play a part in the big picture?

Notes

_____

_____

_____

_____

_____

_____

Quality and Quantity

CHAPTER 4

Quality and
Quantity

LETTER 10:
I WAS CALLED STUPID, DUMB, OR STUPID F***ING GINGER 307 TIMES

"ZACH"

Dear Reggie,

    I Zach would like to thank you for coming to X Middle School. You really did change my life. I am a redhead and the first year I moved here (December of 201X) I was made fun of. In the first week I counted 307 times I was called: A) stupid ginger B) dumb ginger and C) stupid f***ing ginger. 307 times. . . . I contemplated running away but I don't know what happened to make me stay, your speech today really really helped my morale, it is just nice to know I am not the only person who has been made fun of. Thank you so much, I now know there is going to be more meaning in my life and I can make sense of what's happening now in the future.

    Thank you so much brother,
    Zach

Reggie's Reply to Zach

Dear Zach,

When I was in the sixth grade, I was called Fat Albert 281 times in one day. I'm kind of glad to know I'm not the only one who counts things like that. But my adoptive father changed my outlook on the whole thing by telling me something so simple: "They call you Fat Albert because they are jealous. You got a cartoon, and they got nothing!" Zach, I believe they make fun of you because everybody wishes they had the hair color you have.

I went to the University of Tennessee (UT) in Knoxville for my first year of college. I was born and raised in Knoxville. Needless to say, I am a huge Tennessee Volunteers fan, and ginger is one of the greatest colors on the planet! Okay, I'm just saying I'm jealous. I wish my hair was even close to UT orange.

You see, a different perspective can change everything. Zach, you are who you are, and you can't change that, but neither should you want to. The world needs you just the way you are— even with all the flaws, if you want to call them that. To me, your hair color is far from a flaw. I'm just saying.

And I'm not the only one. I look out at so many big crowds all over the world, and I see thousands of people who spray paint their hair the color yours is naturally. So one man's horrible thing is another man's "I wish I could have" thing. Have you seen me? I'm bald! I would take a hair color of any kind right now. Again, I'm just saying.

My point is simply this: you *are* great, and you are *going to be* great—period. No matter the color of your skin. Big or little. Tall or short. Orange, brown, or purple hair. It does not matter to me, so don't let it matter to you either. No matter who you are, you are made just the way you are so the world will be a better place. We just need you to stay in it and be different.

So just shine—just the way you are. Keep going, my brotha, because you're awesome!

I Got Yo' Back!

Reggie Dabbs

LETTER 11:
PEOPLE CALL ME A BABYKILLER

"HAILEY"

Dear Reggie,

I hope you get the chance to read this. I am 17 years old and a senior at XX high school. A few days ago I was ready to end my life. A guy that I have spent two years on broke my heart and told me I was a slut and a dumbass and told me he hated me. I was hurting so bad I carved what he said to me in my arm. I look at the scars as a reminder of the pain he caused. I was pregnant last year with his child and he left me and said the baby wasn't his. I felt alone and scared and the baby wasn't developing right and I got preclampsia. I had an abortion. People call me a babykiller . . . they don't understand that I lost a child. I feel like I'm in a hole that I can't get out of. My family doesn't have money for me to get treatment. I don't know what to do. Well here's the poem I wrote.

A heart that once had a beat
A pair of eyes that once were bright
A soul once so clean and neat
A smile once shown with light

A life filled with hurt and pain
A body beaten and left as a bruise
A broken mind never fully sane
A battle fought an added lose

A deep cut on her precious skin
A thousand tears forming a pool
A loss for life, for death a win
A stupid girl, a b****, a fool

A father's complete absence
A mother's cruelty
A step father's rape presence
A life check, a reality

Reggie's Initial E-Mail Response to Hailey

Dear Hailey,

It hurts me to read the words in your e-mail, but I am so happy that you shared this with me. See, I believe we all are on a path. Sometimes we think we are alone, but we look up, and someone is walking with us. Today that was me on your path and you on mine. You helped me keep on stepping. I hope I did the same for you. Please remember there is a reason for the pain, a reason for the shame, a reason for the hurt. We just have to hold on for the answer. I will hold on with you.

I Got Yo' Back!

Reggie Dabbs

Hailey's Reply to Reggie

The pain is indescribable. I cry every night and pray that I don't wake up the next day. What life is this? Not one I want to live.

Reggie's Reply to Hailey

Dear Hailey,

The first thing I want to say is, I'm sorry. I'm so sorry for your loss and your pain. I was in Ireland on a school tour, and I was leaving one school to go to the next when a girl yelled out at me, "If you could have any superpower, what would it be?" I stopped and looked at her. "I would have the power to take away your pain."

I wish I had the power to take away your pain, but I can't. I want you to know that words do hurt. Words cut so deep, and sometimes we feel we can never ever forget them. In your poem you said that you have a broken mind. Maybe so. But I believe time heals wounds, and time heals words. Out of all the words that can hurt and cut down, causing us to bleed on the inside, I believe there is one word that can heal everything: *love*.

Love can change it all. Even words such as *rape*. Yes, love can change that. Words that make us feel like we can't move or even breathe, but love can make us breathe. So I just want you and every other person out there who feels like this—who writes poems like this—to know one thing: I love you. The fat, black man loves you, and we are going to make it. So never ever give up. Keep breathing. Keep breathing.

I Got Yo' Back!

Reggie Dabbs

Hailey's Reply to Reggie

Hi Reggie,
I thought I was doing better but a few nights ago I broke down and caved in and went back to my old habit of cutting. After I cut I felt better. Then today I had an anxiety attack that turned into rage and I broke my hand from punching holes in things. I don't know how to fix my problem. I feel like I am falling apart and I'm stuck living a life I don't want to live.

Reggie's Reply to Hailey

Dear Hailey,

Some days we wake up and think that we have taken twenty steps backward. We think we are so messed up that we could never recover. But no matter how many times you wake up to find yourself back in that horrible place again, you have to remember that you are still waking up! You are still alive and breathing.

Even if you have taken ten steps backward—broken hearts, even broken bones—you are capable of making those steps back up. If you will just keep living, then your hand will heal. You can redo a wall, but you can't redo a life.

Hold on! Fight for your right to survive. Fight for your right to live. Fight for your right to be happy because happiness is coming; you just have to be here when it arrives. Never give up.

I Got Yo' Back!

Reggie Dabbs

LETTER 12:
MY DAD SAYS I DON'T DESERVE A BIRTHDAY

"JASMINE"

Dear Reggie,

My name is Jasmine. You spoke at my high school last week. Xville. I sat close to the back so you probably didn't really see me. I wore the grey hoodie, if you noticed the 3 girls one was crying that was my friend D. I was very close to crying. I thank you for coming to my school. I almost started crying when you were telling the story about the girl who cut herself. I tell you that to tell you my story.

About 3 years ago, I started having problems with my stepdad. I was really stressed out and I picked up the habit of smoking cigarettes. Well, I got caught smoking, and got in trouble. I tried to tell them why I started smoking. No one listened. A couple of weeks went by and my birthday was the next Thursday, Oct. XX. Well on my birthday, I called my dad and just wanted to talk to him and my stepmother were going out to eat. I asked them if I could go with them since it was my birthday. He told me I didn't deserve anything for my birthday and that I didn't even deserve a birthday.

When he got done telling me that he said he had to go when he hung up he didn't even wish me happy birthday or he loved me. I was crushed. So after that I laid on my bed crying thinking about all the things going on in my life. It was too much for me, I figured everyone would be happy if I was gone, so I went into the bathroom and busted a razor open and tried to kill myself. If my mother hadn't seen my cut mark, I probably wouldn't be here. I still have problems to this day with my father.

I now live with my father. To me he's not much of a father. I am sixteen, I was a unsecure person back then. I have basically raised myself. I love my mother, she's the only thing I really have in my life.

Your friend,
Jasmine

Reggie's Reply to Jasmine

Dear Jasmine,

The first thing I want to say to you—in writing so that forever everybody will know I said it—is:

Happy Birthday to you!
Happy Birthday to you!
Happy Birthday dear Jasmine!
Happy Birthday to you!

(Can you hear my beautiful voice singing through the pages?)

I know many people in the world have had that song sung for them, but, Jasmine, we wrote it in the book for you. Why? Because that's how special you are. I know sometimes you get overlooked. Sometimes people are forgotten by those who should never forget. But Jasmine, we are not going to forget. You are not overlooked.

I am so glad your mom saw your cut before it was too late. We see it every day in someone's life. We catch glimpses of the scars. We don't always know their names, but we see them. We see you. And I know we can't call you out by your real name in this book, but when I met you that day in your school, I saw you. I did not know then that your name is Jasmine, but I cared then, and I still care now.

Many times people will not know your name, but they will still reach out to try to help you. Jasmine, I want you to know that when you felt so lost—you didn't know me, and I didn't know you—there was a coach in your school who knew you. He was the one who made the phone call asking me to come to your school.

There are principals and teachers who know you; they are friends to you even though you may not think of them in that way. You see, they brought me to your school, hoping I would be able to help you. Hoping someday you would realize that somebody really does care.

And it worked! You did realize it, and that's why you wrote us. Your problems may not be gone because you know we care, but knowing it is the first step to breathing another day—because another day will bring another chance to live and see your circumstances change for the good.

So listen very carefully—you will always be loved. And all those birthdays that everybody forgets, you will remember that your daddy, Reggie, put it in his book. Happy birthday, Jasmine!

Never give up!

I Got Yo' Back!

Reggie Dabbs

EXHALE 4:
SILENCING MOUTHS OR CHANGING MINDS

Can you even imagine what it feels like to count the number of times someone calls you an insulting name—and to count past three hundred? Or can you imagine pain so great that you carve words into your arm? Maybe you know all too well.

One of the reasons Reggie is so effective at helping heal the hurts of so many people is that he has faced so much hurt himself. It is easy to think of only the big parts of his story—the shame of being born as the result of a twenty-dollar bill, being given up by his biological mother, living life not knowing the identity of his biological father. If we are not careful, we might inadvertently ignore much of the stuff from Reggie's life that many normal people face every day. Name-calling. Being made fun of. Life in a confusing teenage world.

I think what we are figuring out through the journey of these letters is that the little stuff is not really that little at all. We do not need to have a dramatically tragic past like Reggie's in order to feel drama or tragedy. Those seemingly minor issues of life can build up inside of us like credit card debt—a little charge here, a little purchase there. No one means to do it, but before we know it, we can find ourselves in a hole of debt from which there is no escape.

This is much like the words we use. They seem so small and insignificant when they leave our lips, but they can accumulate to become the building blocks of everything we believe about life, relationships, and even ourselves. Little words. Big impact.

In Zach's case those little words built up into some pretty big problems, to the degree that he wanted to run away from home to escape them. And take note of the focus of the words used against him: his hair color. Really? Could something so small really become something so big?

Negative words often start off as simple observations about the way someone looks, acts, or sounds. We tend to talk the most about those things that stand out the most to us, especially when those things make us different from one another—speech, height, skin color, clothes.

Negative words are so powerful because they often contain something that is true or at least partly true. There is not one of us on the planet, no matter how popular we were or were not in middle school or high school, who did not walk through the doors of our school with a feeling of insecurity or self-consciousness over something—anything, really. It is just part of adolescence.

To a teenager, that tiny zit in the mirror looks as large and looming as Mount Kilimanjaro about to erupt. That one bit of hair that will not just behave and lie down feels like a giant shark's fin to a teenage girl—she can even hear the ominous theme music from *Jaws* playing every time she walks down the hall. Or perhaps a teenage boy cannot afford the same designer clothes as the popular kids. He views himself as wearing a wardrobe of *rags*, all because of designer *tags*—or the lack thereof.

So when we walk into a situation and are already supercharged with insecurity over whatever—real or imagined—we think we are different from everyone else, and we teeter emotionally, like a game of Jenga waiting to collapse. All it takes is one tiny word or sentence to pull the linchpin block and send our world crashing downward. Maybe these kinds of words are something to which you can easily relate:

> *Wow, nice hair!*
> *What's wrong with your clothes?*
> *Out of the way, f***ing ginger!*
> *You're a slut and a dumb a**!*

Bullying almost always starts with words. Rarely does a person just naturally escalate to physical violence or property damage. Words are the currency of the social economy, and bullies try their hardest to get rich quick at the expense of others.

If words are currency, then we are seriously inflated with negative bills. Excessive negativity devalues our opinion of words, desensitizing us from reality and tempting us to spend more and more negative words. Television, movies, music, and video games do not help the issue. We are accustomed to speaking harsh, violent, and inappropriate words because we hear them all the time in whatever media entertains us.

These are some of the reasons that kids in elementary school and middle school have such an impressively tragic arsenal of words to use against one another at such a young age. Remember that Zach was a middle school student when he was cussed at 307 times in one week just because of the color of his hair. Does this not seem at least a little extreme to you? Many middle school students are still watching cartoons every afternoon—maybe the same kids!

A 2007 Department of Education study showed the incidence of bullying and injury to be almost twice as high among sixth graders as twelfth graders.[1] These kids are not yet able to drive a car, pay taxes, enlist in the military, or get married, yet they are capable of using razor sharp words with such skill that the recipients are cutting themselves, running away, or killing themselves or others. Yes, almost every tragedy can be traced back to seemingly little words that are spoken.

We know one book cannot stop these trends. However, we do believe that one person can influence the trend in his or her circle of influence. Does this sound unrealistic? I submit Reggie as Exhibit A: one person making a difference in people's lives everywhere he steps. And there are many more examples of both adults and kids, some of whose stories we will read about in the coming pages. Your story may not be in this book, but you can be one of the examples.

Words make a difference. That is why Reggie speaks to Zach as he does—not to deny the fact that Zach is different but rather to celebrate it. Being different is not something to be ignored. Ignoring it can inadvertently add to the shame so many feel. Much of modern society's answer to this problem has been to stop acknowledging differences. To never reference someone's race. To make everyone wear the same clothes. But differences are not the problem—how we address the differences is the issue.

Reggie shows up on the scene calling himself fat and black—declaring white kids, black kids, Hispanic kids, Asian kids, and all other shades of ethnicity to be his own children . . . each just a different shade of chocolate. Is this politically correct? Perhaps not. Should everyone try this methodology? Definitely not. However, we must face the fact that being politically correct is not proving to be the ultimate solution. It may be better than nothing, but *silencing mouths* without *changing minds* is only treating the symptoms, not the origin of the problem. What we don't need is fewer words, just more of the right ones.

Silencing mouths without *changing minds* is only treating the symptoms, not the origin of the problem.

Hailey's letter strikes hard at this issue. Reggie helps her with more than just the difficulty of harsh words spoken but also the ultimate tragedy of a life lost—and the life of a baby, at that. If you are anything like me, then your heart breaks for Hailey and the pain she is facing seemingly alone.

Though we will discuss suicide, self-harm, and depression more in the coming letters, for now I must say that the tragedy of Hailey's situation is double for me because people in her life seem to possess the power to help, and they have chosen not to. In fact, they seem to have chosen to do more harm instead. Words such as *babykiller* are not easily forgotten, and the hole that Hailey references in her heart has only deepened with every cruel word spoken.

Reggie speaks what she needs to hear—words of love. But as we follow their discussion, Hailey's responses reveal that Reggie's positive words cannot fix things the first time. And in the case of Zach, being verbally abused with more than three hundred various forms of "ginger" does not magically melt away with one encouraging Facebook "message." Though it sounds strange, what we need is not just *quality* words but also a high, steady *quantity* of them.

Reggie stands out in this world for more reasons than his physical size, his skin color, or even his amazing story. He stands out because of his positive words—and the sheer volume of them he dishes out every day to millions around the world. And look at the results. People are obviously anxious to hear something other than what they hear every day.

Few words in this book are as powerful as Hailey's poem, except perhaps Reggie's words in response to her when she is anguished over her continual relapses into depression, anger, and self-destructive behavior: You can redo a wall, but you can't redo a life. I once heard Reggie say something very similar about getting stuck on roller coasters: They will always fix the ride, but will you still be on it when they do?

We can and must reverse the cultural trends. We must learn how to speak the right things at the right times. Words are like the wind: we can speak a cool breeze or a devastating tornado—the choice is ours. Sometimes words are all we have to give. So think both quality *and* quantity. Try this when you are helping friends, children, or students with problems: imagine that you must speak as many replacement positive words as the negative ones they have already heard, if only just for that day. Since these negative words may have come from others or even themselves, they could be quite numerous.

What we need is not fewer words but more. We need a revolution, a literal reversal of an epidemic wherein people seem to know only how to speak destructive words.

Breathable Moment #4: Words are like the wind: we can speak a cool breeze or a devastating tornado—the choice is ours.

Little words can make such a huge difference. Words like *happy birthday* that Reggie said to Jasmine. Do his few words reverse the horrible words that her dad spoke to her? No, but they still make a difference. They still give someone the breath to the keep hoping, and maybe the hope to keep breathing.

Can change really happen around the world? Who knows? But it can definitely happen in you. Why not start there and see where it leads. Like Reggie, your words might keep someone breathing another day.

SIGNATURE 4:
LEAVE YOUR OWN IMPRESSION

1. Were you shocked at the number of times Zach was called by a derogatory name? Why or why not?

2. Why do you think the problem with bullying is more severe in middle school than high school?

3. In what ways do negative words store up like currency or debt? What negative words are stored up in you?

4. How did you feel when you read what Alexis's dad said about her not deserving to have a birthday? Could you ever be capable of saying something like that to someone you love?

5. Do you think it is true that people need more than a high quality of words, but also a high quantity of them? How does this change your viewpoint of dealing with people in crisis?

Notes

_____

_____

_____

_____

_____

_____

_____

CHAPTER 5

Action and Inaction

LETTER 13:
I WRAPPED A CORD AROUND MY NECK AND ALMOST JUMPED

"KAITLYN"

Dear Reggie,

My name is Kaitlyn. You spoke at my school today and I really enjoyed it. I have been having a rough time at school. There have been rumors going around about me sleeping with someone and cheating on someone else and for a while all of my friends called me a lying whore. The rumors weren't even true and everyone believed them.

They came from a guy that likes me but I don't like him anymore and he got upset and started yelling at me. The rumors got so bad that people were saying I had some STD and all of this stuff that wasn't true. They hurt me so bad I almost killed myself last week Tuesday.

I was about to jump off my bed with a cable cord around my neck because I couldn't handle going to school without crying or worrying what people would say. My cousin killed himself about a month ago to this day. When I was standing on my bed, I thought of how he must have felt. And I can't believe I could have done something to stop him. He was my best friend when I was little.

We played Indiana Jones together. He had a crush on me when we were little even though we were cousins. I even heard his girlfriend looked just like me.

I wish every day that I could go back and ask for his number from my uncle and talk to him, message him on Facebook, anything to maybe help him to feel better. But I couldn't.

I wanted you to know that when I almost jumped, I thought of the same speech you gave, when I was a freshman. I'm a junior now at X high school. I remembered your speech from two years ago. I wanted to thank you for everything you do because I don't know if I would be here today if it wasn't for you. Thank you. God bless. Hope to see you again next year.

Kaitlyn

Reggie's Reply to Kaitlyn

Dear Kaitlyn,

Even though your letter is intense and deals with a lot of crazy stuff, what really sticks out for me are words. Words can do so many things—make people happy. Smile. Laugh. Sad. Mad. In this instance, words can totally change a life.

I've heard that being bullied can change your life forever. Think about that. Saying one negative thing could possibly ruin somebody's life forever. You have to decide which kind of person you are. Each person is either a part of the problem or a part of the answer. There are no bystanders—you are either one or the other.

Your letter said that you were thinking about your cousin and what you could have done for him. I know that it hurts to think about what happened to him, but it is not your fault. He made a tragic choice, and it was his choice to make.

But in the grand scheme, we each should be thinking about how we can help those people who are around us every day. Every day we can be the answer for someone.

I am so glad you realized that your life is more than one bad day. One bad decision. One bad comment. Your life does not have to end over one bad rumor, no matter how many times it is spoken.

Some people in your life have chosen to be part of the problem, but you can choose to be the answer. The one day we choose to be the problem could ruin someone's life forever—as one who almost jumped, you know this all too well. But you made a choice *not* to jump! You made a choice to live and breathe another day.

So every day that we wake up, get out of bed, brush our teeth, gargle from a big bottle of Scope, and take a shower, we must tell ourselves: Today, I am the answer! We should say it over and over again. If we say it enough, we may eventually realize that it is true. And maybe we will even look for ways to help people, to show people love, to let them know that they can make it.

Never give up on love because I promise you, as long as you're breathing, love won't give up on you. Even on your saddest day and in the middle of your toughest fight, you can make it. No matter what, you can make it. Do your best to remember the positive words that people say, even people like me. Remember that we did not spread rumors about you. Instead, we spread the truth: you can make it! So never give up.

I Got Yo' Back!

Reggie Dabbs

LETTER 14:
ALL MY FAMILY SAYS,
"KILL YOURSELF"

"MICHAEL"

Dear Reggie,
You came to my school today . . . XX High, and you really
touched me and that really means a lot before i felt like
nothing then you came to my school thank you!! i really mean
it!!!! you helped me!!!

Reggie's Initial Facebook Response to Michael

Thank you for the message, Michael. It means a lot that you would
write me. I know you looked at me from a distance, but you need
to know that I believe in you. Never give up! Okay?

Michael's Reply to Reggie

I will not give up but it is hard when my own dad told me to drop dead and my sisters keep telling me their lives would be better without me and i dont know what to do i truely dont. and some parts of me keep telling me TO KILL MYSELF! and i dont want to but sometimes that seems like the last resort.

Reggie's Reply to Michael

Dear Michael,

Lots of people hear voices in their heads. I think we have these negative things that come at us when we are at our lowest points. It is not just about the words that enter our minds, but it is more about what we do to answer those words. My mind has taunted me many times: *You need to give up. Why don't you just quit? Why don't you just die?* But what I have told those thoughts is that there is a purpose for my life. There is a reason I'm alive, and I'm not going to give up.

I'm not a million people. I'm just a forty-five minute assembly program or just a book—a voice among many others. I'm just a human being like everyone else. I've said it before, and I'll say it again: everybody has something in their past trying to hurt them. Just like you, everybody, at one time or another, hears the voice that says, "Give up! Give up!"

But we must choose not to listen to those voices and hold on to the belief that even in the darkest night, there is a light. Even in our toughest fight of wanting to give up, there is another voice saying, "No! There's a reason! You can make it!"

The whole reason my friend and I are writing this book is so that young people, parents, and educators can hear the right voices. Yes, this whole project is for you—so one boy will know for sure that he has a reason for living. So one girl will know that what she is going through is not the end of her whole life—just the end of this page. When she turns to the next page, there is going to be something good. The next chapter is going to bring hope.

So for one second, let me be that voice in your head—and this is what I am saying: *You're beautiful. You can make it. There is hope. The answer is there, and you are going to live to see it.* That is what we have to hold on to.

I Got Yo' Back!
Reggie Dabbs

LETTER 15:
I WANT TO MOVE AWAY
AND GROW

"EMMA"

Hey Reggie,

My name is Emma, I am from Northern Ireland. I know you probably dont remember me but i was at XX in Belfast the year you came to talk. To be honest i dont really know why i am writing this email but over the past few days i havent been able to stop thinking about it. Im currently reading your book and its changing my life!

I know you are so busy always travelling around the world giving hope to people like me, who have been crushed and broken in so many ways, so i really do appreciate the time your taking to read this.

Its been on my heart to go away somewhere, to another country to really grow my relationship with God and have a mentor to guide me into what Gods plan for my life is because i really dont have a clue. I dont even know where to begin. But its on my heart to go away, well get away! Like i said above i have know idea why i am writing this email to you but i just felt I needed to and thought maybe you could give me advice.

Thank you for everything. This is one more life that you have changed.

Thank you for your time.

Love, Emma
P.S. I GOT YOUR BACK!

Reggie's Reply to Emma

Dear Emma,

Thank you for your e-mail. I want you to know that I did read it, and I am responding to you. I think you're worth it.

You mentioned several things that I think are really important. First of all, it is very interesting that you would mention your relationship with God to me because I never say anything about God or faith when I speak in schools. But since my heart is to respond to you and meet you where you are, let me just say thank you for sharing your heart. Everything that matters to you matters to those who care about you, and I am definitely one of those people. Again, even though I do not talk about it in public schools, like you, I also believe that God is there and that God can help. In my personal life, if it wasn't for my faith, I don't think I would be here today.

The second thing about your message that stuck out to me is a certain word you used: *hope*. When I was in the fourth grade, one of our vocabulary assignments was about this word. Our teacher made us learn how to spell it, and she made us look up the definition in the dictionary. The last part of our assignment was to ask someone else for their definition of hope and not from a dictionary.

I asked my foster mom about hope, and she said, "Whenever things seem impossible, that word makes them possible. Whenever you can't find a light, that word turns on the light." That was the first time I really began to understand what hope is all about—I'm still learning.

I want you to know that no matter what you're going through, there is hope. I believe that if we reach out our hand, someone will reach down and pull us up. All we have to do is ask. I also believe that once we find hope, we can become hope for other people.

Last year on October 30th, the day before Halloween, I went to the grocery store to buy some bottled water. We all know that in America people go crazy on Halloween. As I came through the checkout line, something caught my attention. I was standing behind a mom and her six-year-old son, who were checking out in front of me. The mom was taking the groceries out of the buggy and placing them on the belt. As the cashier was scanning the items, I watched the little boy's eyes become glued to one of the Halloween displays. Though there were many items hanging there, he saw only one thing: a Batman costume.

He got really loud, really fast. "Mom! Mom! Mom! Mom!"

"What's wrong with you?" she answered.

Then in the deepest voice he could muster, he growled, "I'm Batman."

The cashier started laughing. I started laughing. But the boy was just getting started. "Mom, it's only nine dollars! Nine dollars! Tomorrow's Halloween! I'm Batman! I'm Batman!"

When the mother finished putting all of her groceries on the belt, she got down on both knees and pulled her son in close so he could really see her eyes. She said, "I hope you understand that this is all the money we have. I don't get paid until next week. We have to eat this weekend."

The little boy stared at her for a second. Then pulled her in close and kissed her on the lips. He said, "I understand, Mom. But you need to remember . . ." Then his voice transformed back into a deep whisper, "I'm Batman."

She smiled a weak smile and said, "Son, I'm sorry. I'll make you a costume for tomorrow, but it won't be Batman. There is no way you can be Batman. You'll never be Batman." She paid for her groceries and began to walk away.

I try to live my life by something I call the Ten Second Rule. When I see something that needs to be done, I give myself ten seconds to take action. Ten seconds to give someone hope. Ten seconds to show someone love. The clock started ticking in my head, and as I put that water on the belt, the cashier asked me, "Is there anything else?"

"Can you get me a Batman costume for a six-year-old?" She smiled and ran to get it for me. I caught the mom before she left the store and handed her the bag saying, "Ma'am, you forgot a bag."

She looked inside the bag and saw the costume and then looked me in the eyes. "Why did you do this?" she asked.

"Ma'am, just remember that your son . . . he's Batman!" And I walked away.

After I told my wife what happened, she asked me if I was proud of what I had done. I told her no—it was just that I was able to give someone hope. His mom was doing the best she could, and she understood that it wasn't in her power to change the situation. She did not have the funds to make him Batman, so she wanted him to understand reality. It was just not in her power.

But it was in someone else's power. I do believe there is a power that can make the impossible possible. I'm so glad you have at least a hint of hope because it will make a difference in whatever your dream is for tomorrow, whether you stay in Ireland or travel the world. You wanted my advice, so here it is: go find those mentors to help you grow and become a person who gives hope to others—that is a great dream. Find hope. Grow in hope. Give hope away to others. That's why we go into schools every day, and that's why I so wanted to answer your e-mail.

I Got Yo' Back!

Reggie Dabbs

EXHALE 5:
PROBLEM OR SOLUTION?

Many of the letters we have been reading have dealt with bullying and the aftermath of negative words spoken. We think it is
time to begin making the turn from observation to action. What
do you do when you see someone being bullied? What are the
warning signs of suicidal behavior, and what should you do if
you see them?

Suicide is the ultimate ending to the tragedy of negative
words spoken over time, but rarely do people jump off the bed
with the cord around their necks after one rumor. As we have
already discussed, there is a buildup of negative things that lead
them there.

Cutting and other forms of self-harm are often telltale signs
that people are willing to do drastic things to escape the emotional
pain. Physical pain becomes a release for them—something they
can control amid hundreds of things they cannot control.

Over the years Reggie and I have encountered thousands of
kids who have experimented with cutting. Self-harm can vary

from something as minor as a little scratch to gaping wounds or broken hands from punching walls. It is important that you know what to do when you see signs that others are beginning to harm themselves, even if it seems minor at first. Again, things begin small, but they build up over time, sometimes even leading to suicide.

Self-harm is like a drug. People begin with small quantities and become more and more comfortable and courageous with their actions. What once satisfied them may not satisfy them now. Even if they are only seeking attention and have no real desire to seriously hurt themselves, we must take each and every occurrence seriously.

Yes, there are those who are simply seeking attention, but they should not be ignored. Their tactics to receive this attention could escalate and become more severe and more dangerous. But isn't it bad to give them the attention they are seeking—is this not just reinforcing their behavior?

Yes and no. I think the key lies in what kind of attention you give them. First and foremost, above all else, friends, parents, and teachers must be in the mind-set of saving lives. Preserving breaths for another day. If you react with this as your main concern, then the kind of attention you will be returning for their actions will not necessarily be the kind of attention they are wanting, even though it will be the kind they need.

What do I mean? Consider this scenario. You have a friend who has been dealing with a rumor at school, a divorce at home, or perhaps a bully at school. You begin to notice that he is retreating into himself a lot, which is not the way he normally acts. One day, you are hanging out when his sleeve moves up his arm, and you see self-inflicted wounds on his wrists. What should you do?

He may beg you not to say anything. He may even threaten to stop being your friend if you do. These are very difficult waters to navigate, and I have known countless people over the years who were faced with situations similar to this one.

If you do what he asks and keep things quiet, just play out the worst-case version of this scenario. A few weeks or months pass, and your friend's life continues to worsen, yet you remain silent because of your promise. You do not want to lose your friend over it. But then the unthinkable happens, and you get a phone call that your friend had a day he just couldn't handle, and he decided to take his own life.

First and foremost, above all else, friends, parents, and teachers must be in the mind-set of saving lives. Preserving breaths for another day.

You learn that the parents found scars on the now deceased teen's arms and wrists. Then they make this horrible statement that hits you like a punch in the gut: If only someone would have known he was struggling with this stuff, then maybe he would be alive today.

Someone did know: you. You are the friend who could have said something. You are the lifeline he needed even though he did not want to use it. Again, these are very difficult topics to face, but people are self-harming or committing suicide every day all around us—and in almost every case, someone knew something.

So if you see the signs, you must tell someone who can help. Yes, I know that this may not be the popular thing to do. Yes, your friends may threaten never to speak to you again. But you decide which is worse: they never speak to you again either out of misguided anger or because they are no longer alive to do so.

Like it or not, once you know, you are responsible for your actions. You are not responsible for their actions, but you are responsible for yours. In fact, adults are required by law to report self-harming, suicidal behavior, and homicidal behavior to a parent, guardian, or someone in authority, depending on the situation. I have had to do this many, many times. And yes, many times I was begged not to. Many times I really did not want to report it—I was confident things would turn out all right on their own.

But there is always a worst-case scenario hovering over every situation. If it saves a life, then it is worth the trouble. This trouble is why I said that giving the right kind of attention will usually not reinforce negative behavior. Working with students over the years, I have many times taken such decisive and severe action with their small self-harm experimentations or obvious non-authentic threats of suicide that they never sought attention through this method again. I've contacted parents, police, counselors, and hospitals. The idle, attention-seeking threat was usually no longer worth all the trouble it caused because of my actions.

Our greatest concern is for people who are seriously in danger of doing something they can never take back. Whether they want you to know or take action or not, you may be the only reason they live or die. Take action!

Especially when it comes to the issue of suicide, you must take every idle threat seriously. Tell a parent. Tell a teacher. Tell a counselor. Tell an adult who is in authority. But whatever you do, *do not* keep it to yourself. This is especially true if you notice friends not acting like themselves, retreating emotionally, or speaking of an actual plan of how they would commit suicide. This can include text messages, Facebook "messages," or even "tweets." In these cases, you must act quickly—you may not have much time.

Reggie reveals a crucial truth to Kaitlyn that applies to each of us. You are either a part of the problem or a part of the solution. Seems unfair, doesn't it? You may not be the one starting or spreading the rumor, pushing someone into the locker, or hearing a suicidal confession, but you are still a part of the situation because the situation is humanity. You must choose to add to either the problem or the solution. You must choose.

Do not think your inaction takes you out of the game. Sometimes inaction can be the worst kind of action. Imagine that you are walking out in public and you pass a rough-looking man poking at a little baby with a needle. Imagine you can hear the baby screaming in pain. You are not the one directly hurting the helpless child, but unless you do something to stop the abuse, you are hurting him by allowing it to continue.

Breathable Moment #5: You are either a part
of the problem or a part of the solution.

Well sure! If you say it like that, who wouldn't do something to help? Yet many of us pass by cutters, suicidal people, and those who are being bullied to death and do nothing, say nothing. We do not find help, and thus we add to the hurt. There are no neutral players here; each of us is in this game.

Do not think your inaction
takes you out of the game.
Sometimes inaction can be
the worst kind of action.

Michael's letter reveals someone who is in serious trouble, facing real suggestions of death on every side, even from people who should be helping him live. If you were to come across this situation, you should get a caring and responsible adult, authority figure, or counselor involved. Do not take chances with life—take action.

A few final thoughts about bullying and suicide here. If we are each in the game, then bullying is not just about the 15 percent of kids who are being the bullies. It is as much about the 85 percent of kids who do nothing to stop it.[1] Martin Luther King, Jr., said, "In the end, we will remember not the words of our enemies, but the silence of our friends."[2] *Bullying exists as the result of two equal causes: the actions of a few people and the inaction of the rest.*

We are not saying you should suit up like a ninja warrior and go to war with nunchakus and throwing stars, although if someone's life is truly in danger, physical intervention may be needed. Or it could mean making what may be a difficult phone call so that someone in authority can physically check on an individual considering self-harm. In a bullying situation, adding violence to violence is not the right kind of physical intervention—that will only make matters worse. But you can take a bullying victim by the hand and say, "Come with me—you deserve better than this." Then you can lead him or her to a safe place out of harm's way.

In most cases, all that is needed is someone to speak up, reach out, and take a stand for what is right. If the 85 percent are empowered to take the right kind of action, then the instances of bullying, cutting, and suicide will naturally and dramatically decrease.

Breathable Moment #6: *Bullying exists as the result of two equal causes: the actions of a few people and the inaction of the rest.*

If for some reason you or someone you know is contemplating suicide, let me share some realistic truths about what happens when people kill themselves.

Suicide is not the end of pain. I have taken notice that over the years, students mourn the most when their friends take their own lives, yet ironically, those who have had friends commit suicide seem to be more at risk of doing so themselves. Even though they know what horrors the survivors must face in the aftermath of a friend or loved one's suicide, they somehow think their friends escaped all the pain.

Let me be blunt: suicide hurts—bad. None of the people who have successfully killed themselves have ever come back to tell us otherwise. Sharp blades. Poisonous pills. Lethal firearms. Rough ropes. High buildings. These are all very painful. If you think they will somehow end your pain, you could not be more wrong. They will inflict more pain than you have ever felt in your life.

Suicidal people often think that if they were gone, life would be easier for everyone around them. They begin to think of suicide as something almost noble. But in actuality, suicide is very selfish. It leaves others behind to face unthinkable pain for the rest of their lives. Guilt. Loss. Depression. And, yes, that may be what you think those who should love you but do not show it deserve to feel, but just think for a moment about the long aftermath.

Suicide is a momentary decision for you with lifelong consequences for everyone else. You are denying your future spouse a husband or wife, and your future children a mother or father. Your parents and siblings will live with a gaping emotional hole that will never fully close. Your friends will have to go to counseling—or worse, they may feel so devastated that they try to follow you, thus restarting the tragic cycle all over again. Suicide is not the end of pain; it is the ultimate pain.

It ends one lifetime and drastically alters many others' lifetimes. So do not trade *one moment* for *many lifetimes*. Just like Michael, you can choose to hear other voices besides the ones urging you to end it all. We are those voices, and we are not the only ones. A huge crowd of people, with some people you don't even know, is cheering for you to keep breathing another day. Life is always the better choice. Choose it for yourself and for others.

Breathable Moment #7: Suicide is not the
end of pain; it is the ultimate pain.

SIGNATURE 5:
LEAVE YOUR OWN IMPRESSION

1. Do you know anyone who has self-harmed before? What was that person dealing with that led to this behavior?

2. How can reacting in the right way not reinforce someone's desire to gain attention?

3. Do you agree that in a worst-case scenario, inaction can be the worst kind of action? Explain.

4. Why do you think people hear voices in their heads telling them to hurt or kill themselves, especially if they are hearing voices saying this outside of their heads?

5. In what ways is suicide not the end of pain? For whom?

Notes

_____

_____

_____

_____

_____

_____

_____

CHAPTER 6

Pain and Potential

LETTER 16:
MY GRANDPA SEXUALLY HARASSED ME AND KILLED HIMSELF

"ASHLEY"

Dear Reggie,

Thank you so much for coming to XX High School today! It meant a lot to me and the entire school. You had most of my friends in tears with your amazing and powerful words. I look forward to having you come and you are the best speaker we have ever had!

I am not trying to make you feel sorry for me, but two years ago when I was in middle school and you visited us, it was the year after the summer that my grandpa killed himself. I don't really like to talk about it, but I feel like I can tell you. It started off with me getting sexually harassed by him my entire life, and then after my parents found out, they confronted him and a week or two later he killed himself.

Depression runs in my family, but I thought that I could overcome my sadness and never let depression take over me. I guess I was wrong and soon I found myself cutting on a regular basis and I didn't like it but I felt like maybe it would take my mind off of things. On top of that my best friend left me and made up rumors about me and spread them around school. I knew that I didn't want to leave this world by killing myself, but some days were just so hard to get through that I didn't even care.

I have a loving family and I am blessed to have them, but no one could have helped me since I didn't think that I needed to ruin anyone else's life with my drama or make them feel sorry for me. The day you came two years ago changed my life because you made me realize that even when no one is there, I still can believe in myself and that everyone is here on earth for a reason. I almost killed myself and you made me change my mind.

Depression is an illness, but I know that I am very blessed with a loving family and people do care about me and can help me get through it. I don't know how you changed my mind about life, but you sure did. Thank you more than anything. This past summer, I started again and I had the same feelings as the past. I didn't want to tell my parents or get help from anybody because it made me feel like I was weird and strange and people would find out and make more fun of me. I started hanging out with people that don't make the best decisions and almost found myself making really bad decisions.

Somehow every time that something is really hard in my life or I feel like I want to hurt myself, your story always pops into my head. You have the best attitude and thinking of you and your story is what kept me alive some of those times. After today, you really reminded me that life isn't a game and you don't need lots of friends or people to like you to be happy. Not everything is perfect and I have lots to be thankful for. Every time you give your speeches it makes me cry because I feel like I am an important person and I have a reason to live. Thank you for all you have done. You have changed thousands of lives and you have certainly changed mine. To let you know I do not cut anymore and I am working my way out of my depression.

People still are mean (one kid told me to kill myself a couple days ago) but there are so many people who are kind and caring and feel the same way I do. You have helped me to be a better friend and person, and you have saved my life. You are a hero and I hope you never forget that. Thank you a million times Reggie we all love you!!

love Ashley

Reggie's Reply to Ashley

Dear Ashley,

First of all, I would like to say sorry. Sorry that someone with the name "grandpa" could do something like that to you. I know that the word *sorry* may seem small, but when you know what it is like to hurt, then you also know how much it means to hear those words. I know what it's like to hurt; so I say sorry.

I'm so glad you're still living! Breathing. Working. Making life happen. You are right—you don't need a lot of people in your life to make you happy, but you do need one or two. You have people around you who care. I'm so glad that your mom and dad trusted you and believed you; even though it was a horrific thing, you had to tell them. Thank you for trusting your mom and dad and letting them help you through that situation. Even though it ended in tragedy, your life is still something worth living for. You're right—you do have friends. Remember that to be a friend, you must continue to show yourself friendly.

It makes me so happy that I got to come to see you in middle school and then again in high school. That is what this is all about for me—helping to create a movement where we all are continually helping one another because, just like the *Les Mis* T-shirt that I saw someone wearing at your school implies, sometimes people's lives seem to be tragic stories about losing everything. But just like in *Les Misérables*, people can cry out, "I will come back!"[1]

Your life is the same. You lost so much, but you kept coming back. You could have given up, but you didn't. You kept breathing, waiting for another time—and time changes everything.

I Got Yo' Back!

Reggie Dabbs

LETTER 17:
SOMEBODY DOES REALLY CARE!

"MAKAYLA"

Hey Mr reggie,

Your story really made a diference and made me
think, if you survived what you did than I can to! My
name is Makayla and you came to my school today. It
seemed like any other day, but I don't think everybody
knew what you were about at first but it didn't take too
much time to see you were someone diferent.

I went in foster care when I was almost 2 my mother
got me back when I was almost three and my dad got
out of prison when I was three. But of course that
didn't work out. My mother spent her whole life using
drugs so I was put back into the system. From as far
back as I can remember, I remember being moved
around from home to home in the foster system in a
bunch of diferent cities and states. I never really felt

like I had a home, like I had houses to stay in but never a real home. Believe it or not it got worse.

When I was 9 years, one of the biological sons of my foster parents began to rape me. He didn't stop doing this to me for over 2 years. I can't even count how many times. I lost everything because of him. That was no way for a little girl to have to grow up, but it hapened. When I got a litle bit older, I tried killing myself about 12 times. I turned to drugs, sex and alcohol but nothing seemed to help. I spent my life wanting to just belong to someone who would want me for who I am and not for what they could get from me.

I thought I might get adopted by a bunch of diferent families but every time it almost happened, something changed. I almost had a family so many times, but it just seemed like no one cared. I guess I was too messed up, even though some people definitely got a lot worse lives then me. I don't mean to complain or be ungratful.

Today you showed me that someone does care. I do belong somewhere even if its hard to know where sometimes. And to tell you the truth, you saved my life. Lately I've been feeling again like I've wanted to end it, but what you spoke about today about don't feel guilty and your not broken, it really touched my heart.

Thanks so much Mr reggie for everything you did

for me . . .you really made a diference in my life and in others too!

   Makayla

Reggie's Reply to Makayla

Dear Makayla,

I read this letter, and my heart hurt for you. Your pain. Your sorrow. Your rejection. All the reasons you have to give up—for all of these, I am truly sorry. I want you to survive the pain. If you can just make it through the hurt, there is hope at the end of every rainbow—even if you have to endure a hurricane to reach it.

Even though you had to go through hurt after hurt and home after home—even though your story sometimes reads like a horror movie—here you are. You never gave up.

Somebody loves you. Where is your story going to take you? I don't know, but I guarantee you that you will be able to give hope to other people. To give love to other people. You will be there for other people because you never gave up.

So no matter how dark your night is, you must continue to never give up. You have already proven that you can make it through anything; so keep going. The tears may be so many that you think you can't cry anymore, but you will. Never give up. This life is all we have right now, and it's worth living. I applaud you for never giving up. Even when you thought it was over, there was something there to keep you from quitting. I believe in hope. I believe there is something there that will keep you alive until the answer comes.

From one foster kid to another, you are loved. Your story pushes me forward to keep offering hope to the hundreds of thousands around the world living lives like the one you are living. Now your story will keep one of them breathing another day. Your life is making a difference right now. Thank you for sharing it with me.

I Got Yo' Back!

Reggie Dabbs

LETTER 18:
MY MOM ALMOST TOOK MY LIFE

"ELIZABETH"

Dear Reggie,

How are you? My name is Elizabeth. I'm not really sure what to talk about or if you even read this, but I am doing good. I guess I'll tell you about my life. I don't tell many people. I have four brothers but I say five because my brother X's friend live with us a long time and I grew up with him. No sisters and I am the youngest.

My dad is great. I don't have to say anything about my mom. In fact a year ago this week is when she tried to kill me. She cheated on my dad a lot and I always took up for her. When I was little I would lie for her and make up stories for her. I guess I thought that would make her love me.

The older I got the more she began to hate me. I am not sure when I started to notice, but I think she just liked to see me cry. My dad worked a lot so he was never home. I was in middle school, I only got to see him on Christmas. X made a point not to be home. I don't remember my brother Y being around either. Z was always in his room playing games.

My mom and I would always go to a party one of those parties that [last] for a week or so. I bet you were thinking my dad should know something because work don't take that much time. He's a truck driver LOL. Never home still to this day.

A year ago I stood up to my mom and told my dad what a whore she was and she almost took my life. If it wasn't for my dog, I might not be writing this letter. I hate her more than words can say. I only wanted her love. Something I'll never get. Even though I hate her I miss her.

She's my mother, my only mother and I'll never have another one, so there's always going to be a hole in my heart.

Elizabeth

Reggie's Reply to Elizabeth

Dear Elizabeth,

Thank you so much for your letter. I know it's hard to write words like that, but I need you to understand that sometimes even the thing we hate the most is what we also love the most. I know that sounds like a contradiction, but often family can be the thing that hurts us the most. Yet it's also the thing we desire and want the most.

You have to remember my story and how I grew up in foster care. Even though I didn't know my mom, and I've never even seen my father, I still love them to this day. I still love them because that is something that will always be in me. Sometimes I wonder, *Is there something wrong with me . . . that I want to be hated? That I want this sorrow in my life?*

No, it's just human nature. I need to let you know this, and it's very important for you to understand: it's not your fault. Whatever your mom and dad have gone through—to everyone reading this right now—it's not your fault. If your parents have broken up, if one of them has had an affair, you need to know that you still have your own chance to do things right. To have a good family. To love that one person and never hurt him or her in the way your parents have been hurt. To fight for what's right.

So always remember the hurt you have gone through so that when you get older and you have kids—when you are the mom or dad—you'll remember the hurt you have gone through and never duplicate it. A lot of people end up making the same mistakes their parents made. In fact, many won't even try because they think they are going to end up just like their moms or dads.

That's not true! You are your own person, no matter what you have experienced growing up. When you get older, you will get to break that chain. I call it a chain because to me that's what it is. I have heard many people say that if you have never had a mother or father, you will never be a good mother or father. That's wrong! My son is in college, and I love him with all of my heart. My wife and I have been married for more than twenty years now, and it's better than ever. Why? Because we decided that it wasn't going to be that way for us—and it won't be that way for you.

So you keep your head up, no matter what's happening. No matter what they say about your dad or your mom, you keep your head up. Why? Because you are the most perfect you there will ever be—and I like you!

I Got Yo' Back!

Reggie Dabbs

EXHALE 6:
DOMINOES, DEPRESSION, AND FAMILY

For me, these three letters are almost too difficult to read. I was barely able to write some of this without tears. As Reggie says, these kids have so many reasons to give up.

Ashley's letter puts our discussion squarely in the middle of some pretty huge issues: sexual abuse, family communication, suicide, and depression. How do we deal with issues like these, even if they are not as crazy or seemingly as tragic as the stories in these letters?

For starters, Ashley did exactly the right thing in her situation: she spoke up. Much like the issue of suicide, if you or someone you know is being sexually harassed or molested, the time to speak up and report it is now. In this case, it is doubly tragic that Ashley faced something so horrible at the hands of someone she should have been able to trust: her grandfather.

I wish I could tell you that family is always a safe place from sexual, physical, verbal, or emotional abuse, but this is simply not the case. We must be careful here not to go overboard. The vast majority of parents and grandparents out there are completely trustworthy and would never do anything to hurt or abuse their children. There is a reason they are legally called guardians—most of them will lovingly and even violently guard their children with their own lives. Parents are not without faults, but most of them love their children very much even if they do not always know how to show it in the best way.

But there are anomalies. There are those who, for whatever reasons, cross the unthinkable lines and do unthinkable things. If you ever witness or hear about something such as this, you must tell someone. Remember the worst-case scenario from the letter in the previous chapter—you never know what devastating action your inaction might initiate.

Listening to people, especially younger people in situations like these, has shown me a few things about how people deal emotionally with the whole process. I cannot count the people who have sat in my office with knowledge about a certain situation, torn over the question of whether to tell or not.

It is very simple for me to say, "Always tell." But in real life, it is not so simple. As we see in the case of Makayla's letter, the information we are dealing with here could remove someone from their family for the rest of their lives. People could go to jail, run away, or commit suicide. I wish I could tell you that telling always brings about an easy outcome, but this is simply not true.

Sometimes it really hurts to help people. We have heard

again and again that hurting people hurt people. This is true, but we would like to add another truth to this adage: hurting people can still help hurting people. What is difficult does not have to prevent us from doing what is best. We can be hurt and still help those who are hurting.

No one wants to be the cause of such things. No one wants to be the first domino that starts the downfall of the rest. So many times the people being abused or their friends, who know they are being abused, keep quiet for fear of initiating a sequence that can never be reversed.

Breathable Moment #8: Hurting people
can still help hurting people.

There is a lot to address here, but the first truth we can observe is this: we must never lie about things like this. There have been too many instances in our culture where a drama-ridden teen or a jealous friend has made false accusations in order to get revenge or do harm. Accusations about sexual abuse or physical abuse are almost impossible to erase—this is not some movie or high school gossip game. We are not spreading rumors about the cheerleader who called us fat. No, this is life and death stuff. So rise above the immaturity and never make a false accusation in a passing single moment of being a teenager that could affect someone else's life, marriage, career, or family for decades to come.

Beyond that, though, what should you do when the abuse is

real? Do you really want to be the whistle-blower who gets someone thrown in jail or your friends removed from their homes? Do you really want to be the cause of all that?

Let me answer these questions with a crucial truth. In situations of abuse or neglect, sexual or otherwise, those of us who step in to help are not taking the first action in the sequence of events. We may feel as if we are the ones starting the chain reaction, but in actuality the abusers' actions are the ones that have initiated the snowball rolling down the hill. We must have the perspective to realize where we are in the sequence—and to see that it is not at the beginning.

I have been begged by families to just keep things quiet—even treated with hostility and told things like, "You are going to ruin everything!" In these heated moments, it is easy to believe that my actions are causing these problems. But the truth is that my actions are actually *reactions* to *their actions*. I am only taking the best action I can in response to the actions the abusers have chosen.

When we do what is right to call attention to someone in trouble, we must not feel responsible for the aftermath. The arrests. The court dates. The foster care stories. No, none of these things are pleasant, and none of us wants to set them in motion, but again, we are not the ones who set them in motion—the abusers are. Again, I am not attempting to overlook or diminish the devastating pain of all these situations. I am simply saying that when someone speaks up about a legitimate abusive situation, he or she is not the cause of the situation . . . the abuser is.

Humans are creatures of familiarity, and sometimes they will illogically prefer a horrible situation, one that is predictable, to an unknown situation they cannot predict. In other words, they will choose to stay in an abusive home because at least they have a home where they know what to expect. As Elizabeth laments in her letter, she still feels drawn to her mother even though her mother almost killed her.

It is a very odd thing, but often those who are being abused will be the ones who beg you the loudest to keep quiet. They will look at you with a black eye and beg you not to tell—even threatening to stop being your friend. "You will ruin everything!"

But you must see the truth through the emotional fog. The person who punched your friend in the eye is the one who is ruining things, not you. You did not create this fog, neither are you responsible for it—unless you choose to do nothing. People in caskets can no longer ask for help. That is why sometimes we have to help, even when it is not asked for.

These are some of the practical and legal parts of what we should do in situations of abuse or neglect, but there are also a lot of other things to take away from these two letters. The first has to do with family.

Ashley had a set of parents whom she could trust with horrible information—and they acted on it. They believed her. Though we are showing you so much tragedy in these letters, here is a glimpse of light. Most parents will listen and defend their children. Family is not the enemy; family should be a safe place, even if it is not biological.

Secondly, notice that even though Ashley had parents she could trust, she still faced a battle with severe depression. Depression is a buzzword we hear every day in our culture. Sometimes people use the word *depression* when they are really just having a bad week. Self-diagnosis has become rampant, but true clinical depression is real and requires a real doctor or professional to diagnose.

In many cases, doctors seem to have overdiagnosed. Perhaps they do so because it is too difficult and time-consuming to teach people how to cope with the ups and downs of life. A pill taken in two seconds is much easier to swallow than a plan that takes months or years to adjust to.

We are not denying the existence of depression or the need for medicinal intervention; we are merely stating that every time you feel tired, hungry, or go through a season of stress, you are not necessarily experiencing clinical depression. Sometimes you are just experiencing life. Your first method should be to try and face it and get through it by developing healthy mental, physical, and emotional coping skills—you are stronger than you think.

But, as in Ashley's case, there are instances when depression is very real and an issue cannot be worked through without professional help. In these cases we need the help of family, physicians, counselors, friends, and perhaps even medication. But much like everything else we have written about, one word, one counseling session, one day, one pill, or one day at the park may not necessarily fix everything instantaneously. Even professionals should not be expected to fix depression in a day. You can still keep working on your coping skills even while you are being treated by a doctor or psychologist.

If you do need professional help, or you have a friend, child, or student who does, there should be no stigma involved. As Ashley pointed out, depression is an illness, and like all illnesses, there is not always a formula for how we deal with it. Sometimes it may last a week; sometimes it may last a year. It may be triggered by something tragic, or it may be triggered by something you ate. It may require medication, or it may require more sunlight and some exercise. But do not feel like an outcast because you face depression—illness is part of being human, so do what is necessary to deal with it without any shame. You should not feel ashamed to be human.

As I stated way back in the prologue to this book, we are not trying to give every answer to every problem from every life of every person. There are not enough pages on the planet for this. But for me, these three letters are worth rereading even though they are difficult to process. Why? Because they show us the realities hidden in plain sight all around us.

And when we are aware and even looking out for those in trouble, then perhaps we can see what everyone else is missing. Perhaps we can keep someone from being abused or raped. Perhaps we can reach out to others dealing with depression before they descend into thoughts of suicide. Perhaps we can adopt or foster kids in trouble to make their experience the opposite of the horror stories we have just read.

For Reggie, that's just what happened—his tragedy was

transformed by the love of a family. Family does not have to be biological; it doesn't even have to be legal. Family can simply be a place of acceptance, safety, and love. It is not a place where you can do whatever you want without consequences. Family will love you enough to call you out when you do wrong. Hold you accountable and responsible for your actions. Empower you to grow into a better person. Be willing to argue appropriately and say things that are hard to hear but needed.

Family does not have to be biological; it doesn't even have to be legal. Family can simply be a place of acceptance, safety, and love.

This is family, and everyone needs one. So no matter who you are—young or old—perhaps it is time to *be* what everyone, including you, needs the most: family. You never know whose life it might spare from the unthinkable.

SIGNATURE 6:
LEAVE YOUR OWN IMPRESSION

1. Compared to the other letters you have read so far in this book, what were your reactions to the letters from Ashley, Makayla, and Elizabeth?

2. Is it easy to become desensitized when you have read about so much tragedy? If you consider the fact that for every letter Reggie and John have used in this book there are a hundred more just like it, what is your natural reaction?

3. Why is it even more tragic when sexual or physical abuse comes from a family member? Why is it so important to tell the truth about matters such as these?

4. Why do you think it is easy for people who speak up for someone else in trouble to feel responsible for setting a series of events in motion? Are they really responsible? Who is?

5. How would you define family? Is a biological component required?

Notes

_____

_____

_____

_____

_____

_____

CHAPTER 7

Entitlement and Empowerment

LETTER 19:
I WAS ALMOST ABORTED, AND MY DAD LEFT

"ZOE"

Dear Reggie,

Hi, my name is Zoe and you have inspired me and encouraged me to keep moving on and not to give up. I hope you have the time to read this because it would mean a lot to me if you did.

I'm a freshman in XX high school and I enjoyed your assembly. Before it started though I heard people talk about a "bullying assembly" and I rolled my eyes and thought not another one, nothing ever works at our school no matter how many work sheets, posters, assemblies it will never change. Then I walked into the gym and sat down and was blown away!

I wanted to slap myself for thinking the worst! I sat through your talking and thought this guy is amazing and

I admire him and you totally changed my perspective of things like super heroes and how no matter what crap was in their past they still moved on and became who they were "an amazing super hero". I have learned so much today and hope to see you come back again. You really touched me with your story.

My mother was also a teenager when I was conceived totally unplanned and I was almost aborted my dad left 2 years ago it still hurts. Today you helped me see that those things don't define me they help me to see who I really am!

Thank you a Million times over and over I will never forget this day.

Reggie's Reply to Zoe

Dear Zoe,

Thank you so much for your letter and for sharing part of your story with me. The reason I talk so much about superheroes is because I meet them every day in schools and assemblies all around the world.

The amazing thing about superheroes is that most of the time no one knows their true identity. They are hidden in plain sight. In fact, sometimes they are the very people we overlook or even make fun of. If you think about it, Clark Kent and Peter Parker were both pretty big nerds on the outside, but there was so much more to them than what anyone could see. And they each had a backstory that was easy to overlook.

We often overlook people's backstories too—and we miss the superhero inside of them. We see kids dressed funny, and so we make fun of them. We have no idea that they have no money and that those are the only clothes they can afford to wear.

We hear a guy with a speech impediment, so we laugh and say he sounds like Bugs Bunny or some other cartoon character. We don't know that he had to endure throat surgery because of the cancer that attacked his body. He could have died if they had not performed the surgery, but all we do is make fun of his speech.

You said that I changed your perspective about your own backstory—that's great! Now we have to keep going to get everyone around us to change the way we do things. Young people who are being made fun of are literally to the point where they are taking their own lives. We are killing the superheroes.

Not long ago in Mississippi, a little girl on a bus was told she was ugly and that she should die. She wrote a note to her mother and then purposely walked in front of a car. It's just not right! It's not fair! Everyone should have a chance to be loved. It's time to train ourselves to think about other people.

Not too long ago, I happened to be walking down the street behind a man I did not know. He came upon a homeless lady who was begging in the street. When the man walked by her, he looked at her and said, "Get a job."

When I walked by her, I gave her five dollars. What makes

people say, "Get a job," when for all we know, the situation may not be quite that simple? Why don't we think of the lady as someone's daughter, someone's friend, someone's family member? We've got to be able to take care of one another, or the world will never become a better place. It will only get worse.

I'm glad you listened to me today. I'm glad I was able to help your school. But *you* have to help your school as well. As I told you about the superheroes, you are the answer. There are two types of people in the world: you are either a part of the problem, or you are a part of the answer.

I am a part of the answer, and so are you. Thanks for caring. Thanks for being the hero.

I Got Yo' Back!

Reggie Dabbs

LETTER 20:
I LOST MY LARGE INTESTINE . . . AND I WANT TO LOSE MY LIFE TOO

"SAMANTHA"

Dear Reggie,

I just wanted to say thank you for coming to XX high school today. I know you receive a large amount of e-mails and I appreciate you taking the time to read mine.

Another reason why I wanted to write you an e-mail is I was hoping you can help me. When I was seven years old I was diagnosed with ulcerative colitis. This disease is a type of cancer that almost took my life. I was left with an alternative: have surgery at age eleven or live for only 6 months. I picked surgery of course.

This surgery required me to lose my entire large intestine. After my surgery I was left with a horrible ten inch scar on one part of my stomach and another scar is five inches. I'm eighteen years old today and I have dealt with so much in my life that I would not wish this on my worst enemy.

My main reason why I am writing to you is that I have thought about the big S word (suicide). It's not an option for me anymore because I cannot leave my family to deal with heartache. Plus it is morally wrong. I was hoping you can give me advice so I can feel better about myself and accept myself for my condition. Thanks so much for coming to my school and talking to us. I hope you and your wife are well.

Sincerely,

Samantha

Reggie's Reply to Samantha

Dear Samantha,

I remember meeting you at your school. When I was young and just out of college, I started traveling to speak at schools. I had the opportunity to meet a very cool man whom a lot of people called a great American hero. His name was Dave Roever.

Dave was a Vietnam veteran, and I traveled with him for about seven years, speaking at schools all over the world. During the war, he had a hand grenade blow up six inches from his face—it literally burned his face off. If you Google his name, you will see what I am talking about; the whole right side of his face was scarred very badly.[1]

One day we went to a high school, and as we walked in, I could hear some kids making fun of him. He ignored them and kept walking. When he got up to do the assembly program, he said these words: "My scars are on the outside, but your scars are on the inside. Love can make our scars go away."

That was all I could think of when I read your letter—love can make our scars go away. Always remember that someone loves you just the way you are. Somebody will see past your scars and see who you really are.

After the assembly that day, Dave and I were about to leave when a young girl walked up and asked him, "Can I touch your face?" He agreed, and when she touched his mauled skin, she said, "I don't see scars; I see a prince."

That's what you are! You may not realize it today, but all the pain you are going through right now is preparing you to be the answer the world has been looking for tomorrow.

Your pain is not meaningless—your willingness to endure it makes you a hero. So hold on because somebody is going to love you just the way you are.

We all have scars, but we all have something else more important: love. Just keep breathing another day so love can get to you. Never give up.

I Got Yo' Back!

Reggie Dabbs

LETTER 21:
MY NAME IS UNNEEDED (WRITTEN JUST MONTHS BEFORE A SHOOTING AT HER SCHOOL)

"OLIVIA"

Dear Reggie,

My name is unneeded because its in my e-mail but I just wanted to sincerely thank you for coming to my school. I really appreciate talking to you. You helped me to realize that from all the stuff that I have been through im not going to make the same bad choices that ive made in the past.

You have helped me before you even came to my high school (XX high school). I have watched a few of your speeches and honestly your words have stopped me from doing something that could have ended my life. You are an amazing speaker and i love you for what you do and

the great hug you gave me. And Mr. Whitechocolate is an
awesome nickname. I would appreciate a reply.

With much love,

Olivia

Reggie's Reply to Olivia

Dear Olivia,

Thank you so much not just for e-mailing me, but also for listening to my words in the assembly and on YouTube—and for letting me give you a hug. Thank you so much for not giving up, which brings purpose to what I do every day.

There are many times in life that we want to give up. In fact, I heard a song that implies life hurts us so badly sometimes, it can be hard even to breathe. But even though it was hard to breathe, I'm so glad you kept breathing. Breathing means you have a future.

Know that no matter what happens in your future, you made it over this hurdle, so you can make it over the next one too. And remember, I always got yo' back!

I Got Yo' Back!

Reggie Dabbs

EXHALE 7:
HIDDEN SUPERHEROES

As we approach the finish line of our exploration of these twenty-one letters, you may feel a bit overwhelmed with the realities of what this generation is facing. Our goal has not been to depress you or leave you with a feeling of hopelessness but rather to open your eyes to what is happening in your own backyard.

But beyond that, we want to empower you. The war for the lives of this generation is not lost even if it feels as though we are losing. We need you to enlist and take up arms in defense of what matters most: our friends, family, children, and students.

You may be only a teenager yourself, but you can save a life. You can speak hope. You can care enough to ask others about their day. You can do what is right to stop bullying before someone's life is either ruined or lost.

I was moved by Reggie's story about the girl in Mississippi who stepped in front of a car because someone convinced her she should die. What an unnecessary and senseless loss of a beautiful life—and over what? The only redeeming part of her story is that people like Reggie and I are telling her story, and caring people like you are reading it. Her tragedy and the tragedy of every person whose story has been told in this book does not have to be in vain.

We can become desensitized to their stories, or we can become galvanized by them. We can casually observe, or we can actively intervene. We can remain motionless and tend to our own issues, or we can become mobilized as a movement of people with goals and dreams bigger than just our own interests. One girl. One boy. One family. Each of these is worth our time and energy.

I was particularly motivated by Samantha's letter to Reggie. What an amazing young woman! Just consider all that she has faced in her life with the surgeries and the difficult aftermath of living life with no large intestine. If anyone might feel like giving up hope, it would be her. Who could blame her?

Yet in the middle of her letter to Reggie, she declares that though she has been tempted by the idea of suicide, she knows she cannot go through with it because of what it would do to her family. What a mature, noble, and courageous statement to make in the midst of such unspeakable hardship.

If you read these letters and feel hopeless, take heart because Samantha proves to us that there are plenty of superheroes hidden in the hallways of this generation. Young men and women who have been dealt incredibly difficult hands yet keep on breathing and even find ways to think about the welfare of others.

As Reggie points out in telling Dave Roever's story, the deepest scars do not have to take away the beauty of a person's existence.

This generation is full of princes and princesses, even if they don't know it. That is why we are trying with all our might to tell them there is hope, no matter what scars cover their bodies or minds.

Olivia reminds us that for every letter you have read, there are millions of other stories still untold. She states that her name is unneeded, but we disagree. You know the names of others with untold stories. You walk beside them every day through the halls of your school. They sleep in beds inside your house. They turn in papers on your desk. They are your brothers and sisters, your nieces and nephews. And, yes, their names are very much needed in the story of their generation.

Reggie is only one man. I am only one man. This book is only a collection of a few pages with a few words. But collectively, every person out there can have their name known and valued by someone. Please do not let this book be an observational experience for you. Do not read these stories and gasp at the sometimes gruesome details, only to return to your life without making any changes. These stories are not about Martians; they are about humans, people who share the office, the desk, the room, the locker, or even the bunk bed right next to you. Do not let their names go unneeded.

You are the one who decides if new information becomes transformation. To be shocked and remain unchanged would only add to the tragedies. But to be shocked and also move to action would add your name to the list of heroes who already work to save the lives and preserve the breaths of this generation.

Teachers. Police. Parents. Coaches. Volunteers. Counselors. Social workers. Inner-city workers. Club sponsors. The super-heroes are all around you—won't you join them?

You may or may not have noticed that in Reggie's responses to the letters and in my commentaries we have tried to be straight-forward with those in crisis so that they still have choices. At first glance this seems a bit unreasonable and unfair. Why would we challenge those who have already been hurt so badly, often from no actions of their own, to take positive action? Shouldn't we just give them a break?

Trust me when I say that the greatest disservice we could ever do to this generation is rob them of their empowerment to keep making choices for themselves, regardless of what other choices people around them have made that may have deeply wounded them. Like Reggie—like Dave Roever, like Dr. Martin Luther King Jr., like you and me—if we are still breathing today, then we still own our choices today.

We can respond with kindness if we choose, even if we do not feel like it. Yes, we can do it. We can choose to forgive even when the other person does not deserve it. We can choose to fight depression even though it is in our family history. We can choose to stand up for the little guy even though it means we will face trouble for it. We can choose to tell someone that our friend is in trouble even though our friend may not realize for many years that we are saving his life.

Even if all else is taken away, no one can rob you of your choice. Choice is the essence of being empowered. You can choose to stop being bitter. You can choose to go to college. You can choose to refuse to be lazy. You can choose to quit the gang. Listen in class. Love your children. Speak kindly to your students. Reach out to the bully. Refuse the drugs you are being offered. Say no to the boy or girl trying to sleep with you. You can choose, and because of that, you are much more powerful than you might feel.

That is why Reggie and I constantly try to point out to every person we encounter, even persons in tragic situations, that they can still choose to keep breathing until tomorrow. They can be robbed of almost everything else—and, yes, it is a tragedy. But the greatest tragedy of all is when they think that because of the circumstances of their lives and families or because of the choices of others, they can no longer choose to live.

Breathable Moment #9: Even if all else is taken away, no one can rob you of your choice.

Though they may have been victims of real abuse, neglect, or ridicule, they do not have to stay victims forever. Yes, they may always have to live with the realities of their situations, but they are not limited to those situations. Another breath is another moment of hope. Another choice to keep moving forward. Another day to see how the story will continue to play out.

The modern generation often seems to feel entitled. We expect to receive without working to earn it. We demand respect without giving it. We speak harshly to others yet feel slighted when we are spoken to in a like manner. We feel entitled to every benefit, yet we feel released from any responsibility.

This entitlement mentality is poison because it keeps people from owning the power of their own choices. Instead of choosing, they act as if all choices have already been made for them. They become perpetual victims even when there is no reason for it. But the truth is that even when there are valid reasons to feel like the victim, we still have choices to make. We are responsible for not only our *actions* but also our *reactions*.

Please do not misunderstand me or think my words insensitive. As we have read, there are very real victims in our society. People who have been deeply hurt at no fault of their own. But even these people, though they need love and acceptance, do not have to be done living. They do not have to be done choosing. They do not have to be done.

Allowing another person's cruel or tragic actions to define all of someone's remaining personal choices for the rest of his or her life only gives the abuser, bully, or situation more power. We can be sympathetic without inadvertently hurting people worse with the assumption that they must remain victims forever with no choice in the matter. No, we can, instead, listen, love, cry, help, hurt with them and empower them to move on to the next day.

Entitlement produces victims; empowerment produces victors. We believe that you can be a part of the solution and not a part of the problem—and the choice is yours to make.

We choose to see the heroes amid the horrific headlines of our generation. We choose to defend the defenseless and help the weak. We choose to stand up to the bully and see him become a part of the answer. We choose to blow the whistle on abuse and fight the epidemic of suicide. We choose to care enough to listen. To speak truth. To speak love. To speak out.

Will you join us?

Breathable Moment #10: Entitlement produces victims; empowerment produces victors.

SIGNATURE 7:
LEAVE YOUR OWN IMPRESSION

1. In Reggie's answer to Zoe, he talks about how easy it is to overlook someone's backstory by focusing merely on what is seen on the outside. Do you think this happens a lot in modern culture as a whole? Explain.

2. How does reading about Samantha's battle with ulcerative colitis at such a young age make you feel? What do you notice about her outlook despite the many hardships she has faced?

3. How did you react to Olivia's letter, knowing that it preceded a school shooting at her school? How might have things changed if the alleged shooter would have experienced the same changes Olivia did from Reggie's visit?

4. Has this book truly opened up your eyes to what is going on in "your own backyard"? How so?

5. What are three practical ways you can immediately start becoming a part of the solution instead of the problem?

Notes

_____

_____

_____

_____

_____

_____

Endless Ink: An Epilogue

W e began this book describing an unknown pair of shoes walking toward the door that leads to the hearts of this generation. That is where we end as well.

Unknown shoes are still walking even as we speak. No doubt there will be those whose intentions are not pure who fill those shoes. There will always be more tragedy. But if more of us would fill those shoes, then perhaps the top stories we read about will not be those of tragedy but of hope.

Yours are now the unknown shoes that are walking toward that door. Your shoes are filled with the potential to hurt or to heal. To entitle or to empower. To judge or to defend. To believe in or condemn.

This is because your shoes are filled with your own feet. We wrote these words to shine a light on the lives of people in our society today, and we beg you not to turn off that light when you close this book. Leave a lamp burning for the person writhing in the darkness of difficulty or tragedy. Remember, you may be the next one whose eyes sift the darkness in search of just a solitary ray of light.

For when these pages stop turning, the world will continue to turn. Let us again remind you that for every letter we shared, we have hundreds—even thousands—more. Many people, in this very moment, find themselves on the brink of giving up on breath. You know them, even if you don't always know that you know them. Now you know that you know.

For those of us who work with people—and especially young people—in crisis, the task feels overwhelming because the job is difficult, to say the least. It is thankless and endless. Our teachers are underpaid, distrusted, and underappreciated. Counselors and social workers are very much in the same boat. In our culture, if you want to really help those in need, it is not uncommon that you must become a person in need yourself by being willing to work for less pay and with fewer resources. These areas are not always our society's priorities because they are choppy waters— people easily get seasick here.

Yet so many heroes raise the sails of hope every day:

- parents who listen, defend, and love their children
- teachers who keep walking into their classrooms and pouring into the hearts and minds of this generation
- counselors, volunteers, and social workers
- community leaders in local clubs and religious groups

The world may not lack tragedy, but neither does it lack heroes. We thank all of you.

You especially know how overwhelming the problems are, and that we cannot be everywhere at once. But there is more than one thing that is present everywhere these problems exist, even adding the potential to help. Among all that's present, this particular commonality is always near when trouble arises. What is it?

It's the rest of us! People are always standing right there beside people. You do not have to be perfect to help. You do not need to be a professional or have ever worked in the field of social work, counseling, or education. As we said in the first chapter, helping someone starts with caring, not fixing.

The world may not lack tragedy, but neither does it lack heroes.

As the last letter demonstrated, there are things ahead that no one can predict. It may not be a school shooting or some heinous crime of abuse or neglect; nevertheless, there is still ink left in the pen of people's stories. As long as they are writing, you can be writing too—a story of compassion, concern, and care for those around you.

So consider your eyes at least partially open. Do not choose to close them because every time you do, tragedy occurs somewhere in the darkness. We need you to be awake, to be aware, and to be alive so that others can live. We need you to be both breathing and helping those around you to breathe.

The unknown shoes are no longer unknown to you. Now you decide whether a hero or a villain will fill those shoes.

Choose the hero.

Notes

Chapter 3: Bullies and Backstories

1. The Youth Alliance, Living Bully Free, "Bullying," http://livingbullyfree.com/bullying/.
2. The Youth Alliance, Living Bully Free, "Educators," http://livingbullyfree.com/educators/.

Chapter 4: Quality and Quantity

1. The Youth Alliance, Living Bully Free, "Bullying," http://livingbullyfree.com/bullying/.

Chapter 5: Action and Inaction

1. The Youth Alliance, Living Bully Free, "Bullying," http://livingbullyfree.com/bullying/.
2. Martin Luther King Jr., "Massey Lectures," radio broadcast (Canadian Broadcasting Corporation, 1967).

Chapter 6: Pain and Potential

1. Victor Hugo, *Les Misérables*, Charles E. Wilbour, trans. (New York: Random House Modern Library, 1992).

Chapter 7: Entitlement and Empowerment

1. The Roever Foundation, http:// http://roeverfoundation.org /meet_dave_roever.php.

About the Authors

REGGIE DABBS has been one of the most sought-after public school and event speakers in the United States and the world for more than two decades. From professional athletes and stay-at-home moms to high school students, Reggie relentlessly chases his personal passion around the globe by sharing his own astonishing story of tragedy, redemption, and hope with millions of people each year. An acclaimed saxophonist, Reggie lives with Michelle, his wife of more than twenty years, and their son Dominic. He is also the author of *Reggie: You Can't Change Your Past, but You Can Change Your Future.*

JOHN DRIVER MS, is an author, speaker, and fifteen-year community leader, advocate, and mentor. As a former public educator, he has authored or coauthored more than a dozen books. He lives near Nashville, Tennessee, with his wife, Laura, and their daughter, Sadie Jane.

I don't have to know your name to know your pain . . .
I have my own.

I don't have to see your home to know your shame . . .
I have my own.

But someone loved me just the way I am,

and someone loves you just the way you are.

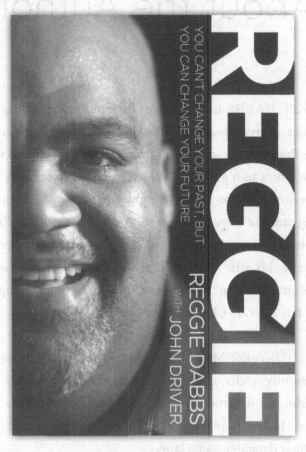

REGGIE

YOU CAN'T CHANGE YOUR PAST, BUT
YOU CAN CHANGE YOUR FUTURE

REGGIE DABBS

WITH JOHN DRIVER

AVAILABLE IN PRINT AND E-BOOK

WHEREVER BOOKS ARE SOLD

What People Are Saying About *Reggie*

"The stories and principles you encounter in this book not only will inspire you but also will lead you on a journey to the core elements of life—and the potential therein to change."

    —MARK BATTERSON

"Every parent, youth leader, and teacher should read this book."

    —ISRAEL HOUGHTON

"Through his fiery, passionate testimony, Reggie has impacted multitudes of lives worldwide while inspiring people to live a life of excellence."

    —JOHN BEVERE

"Reggie Dabbs . . . inspires me with his testimony and ability to reach a cross-cultural generation that is searching for the truth in life. Reggie is absolutely the real deal with a real message of hope!"

    —RICARDO

"Every time I see [Reggie]—whether backstage at a convention center, by chance in an airport, or while he's on stage playing sax—I smile. He's that kind of guy—the kind you can't be around without feeling a bit of sunshine."

    —DAVID CROWDER